COLLINS
Cycling
in
CORNWALL & DEVON

W0009912

HarperCollins*Publishers*

Published by Collins
An imprint of HarperCollins*Publishers*
77–85 Fulham Palace Road
London W6 8JB

First published 1999
Copyright © HarperCollins*Publishers* Ltd 1999
Maps © Bartholomew Ltd 1999

Routes compiled by Neil Wheadon.
Design by Creative Matters Design Consultancy, Glasgow.
Typeset by Bob Vickers.

Photographs reproduced by kind permission of the following:
J. Allan Cash Photolibrary pages 5, 8, 30, 32, 35, 39, 41, 44, 57,
61, 69, 72, 75, 83, 91, 95, 99, 101, 105; Cornwall Tourist Board
pages 22 (David Hastilow), 46; Neil Wheadon pages 65, 107;
Andy Williams pages 11, 15, 18, 36, 49, 53.

The landscape is changing all the time. While every care has
been taken in the preparation of this guide, the Publisher accepts
no responsibility whatsoever for any loss, damage, injury or
inconvenience sustained or caused as a result of using this guide.

Printed in Scotland

ISBN 0 00 448914 4
99/1/14

CONTENTS

KEY TO ROUTES

Route		Grade	Distance km (miles)		Time to allow	Page
1	Wadebridge, Padstow and the Camel Trail	easy	18.5	(11.5)	2–3 hours	14
2	Totnes and the South Devon Railway	moderate	20	(12.5)	2–3 hours	17
3	Perranporth, St Agnes and Penhallow	moderate	21	(13)	2–4 hours	20
4	Okehampton and Dartmoor	strenuous	22.5	(14)	2–4 hours	23
5	Gweek and Goonhilly Downs	moderate	23	(14.5)	2–3 hours	25
6	Redruth and the Mineral Tramways	moderate	25.5	(16)	2–4 hours	28
7	Clovelly and Hartland	strenuous	26	(16)	2–4 hours	31
8	Exmouth and Budleigh Salterton	moderate	26.5	(16.5)	3–4 hours	34
9	Sticklepath, Chagford and Castle Drogo	strenuous	29	(18)	2–4 hours	38
10	Lynton, Lynmouth and the Valley of the Rocks	strenuous	33.5	(21)	3–4 hours	42
11	Roche, St Columb Major and St Mawgan	moderate	35	(21.5)	2–4 hours	45
12	Kingsbridge, Salcombe and Slapton Sands	strenuous	39	(24)	4–7 hours	48
13	The Lizard Peninsula	moderate	40	(25)	3–4 hours	52
14	Tavistock and Burrator Reservoir	strenuous	45	(28)	3–6 hours	56
15	Lydford and Brent Tor	moderate	47	(29)	3–6 hours	60
16	Tiverton and Bampton	moderate	54	(33.5)	3–5 hours	64
17	Tintagel and the North Cornish Coast	moderate	56.5	(35)	4–8 hours	68
18	Bude, Widemouth Bay and Holsworthy	moderate	59	(36.5)	4–7 hours	73
19	Penzance and Land's End	moderate	74.5	(46.5)	5–8 hours	78
20	Barnstaple and the Tarka Trail	strenuous	78	(48.5)	4–8 hours	82
21	Truro and the Roseland Peninsula	strenuous	79	(49)	5–9 hours	86
22	South Molton to Exmoor	moderate	86	(53.5)	5–10 hours	90
23	South Hams and the Plym Valley	strenuous	88.5	(55)	5–10 hours	94
24	Exeter and Honiton	strenuous	93	(58)	6–10 hours	100
25	Coast to coast – a grande randonnée	strenuous	127	(79)	7–12 hours	106

Distances have been rounded up or down to the nearest 0.5km (mile).

Route colour coding

undemanding rides compiled specifically with families in mind
15–25km (10–15 miles)

middle distance rides suitable for all cyclists
25–40km (15–25 miles)

half-day rides for the more experienced and adventurous cyclist
40–60km (25–40 miles)

challenging full-day rides
over 60km (over 40 miles)

grande randonnée – a grand cycling tour
100km (60 miles)

 Routes marked with this symbol are off-road or have off-road sections
(includes well-surfaced cycleways as well as rougher off-road tracks)

Dartmoor

LOCATION MAP

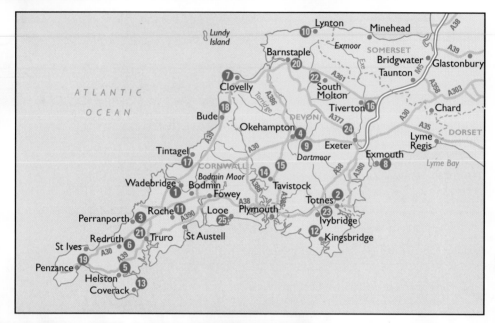

KEY TO ROUTE MAPS

M23	Motorway	▬▬ ▪▪▪▪	Cycle route / Optional route	☎	Telephone
A259	'A' road / Dual carriageway	🚴	Start of cycle route	⅋	Picnic site
B2130	'B' road / Dual carriageway	⑫—	Route direction	⋀	Camping site
	Good minor road	Ⓑ	Place of interest	👫	Public toilets
	Minor road	🍺	Public house	†	Place of worship
	Track / bridleway	☕	Café / refreshments	✹	Viewpoint
—•—	Railway / station	✕	Restaurant	⌐	Golf course
⊥⊥⊥⊥⊥	Canal / river	*i*	Tourist Information Centre	⁙	Tumulus
	Lake	Ⓟ	Parking		Urban area
50	Contour (height in metres)	🏪	Convenience store		Woodland

Height above sea level

50	100	150	200	300	400	500	600	700	800	900 metres
165	330	490	655	985	1315	1645	1975	2305	2635	2965 feet

INTRODUCTION

How to use this guide

Collins' *Cycling in Cornwall & Devon* has been devised for those who want trips out on their bicycles along quiet roads and tracks, passing interesting places and convenient refreshment stops without having to devise their own routes. Each of the 25 routes in this book has been compiled and ridden by an experienced cyclist for cyclists of all abilities.

Cycling in Cornwall & Devon is easy to use. Routes range from undemanding rides compiled specifically with families in mind to challenging full-day rides; the type of route is easily identified by colour coding (see page 5). At the start of each route an information box summarises: total distance (in kilometres/miles – distances have been rounded up or down throughout to the nearest 0.5km/mile and are approximate only); grade (easy, moderate or strenuous based on distance and difficulty); terrain; an average time to allow for the route; directions to the start of the route by car and, if appropriate, by train.

Each route is fully mapped and has concise, easy-to-follow directions. Comprehensive information on places of interest and convenient refreshment stops along each route are also given. Accumulated mileages within each route description give an indication of progress, while the profile diagram is a graphic representation of gradients along the route. These should be used as a guide only.

The following abbreviations are used in the route directions:

LHF	left hand fork
RHF	right hand fork
SO	straight on
SP	signpost
TJ	T junction
TL	turn left
TR	turn right
XR	crossroads

Cycling in Cornwall and Devon

The rides in this book run through Devon and Cornwall, taking in Exmoor, Dartmoor and Bodmin Moor, the surrounding countryside, and the coasts, from Exmouth and Lynton in Devon, down to the Lizard Peninsula and Land's End in Cornwall.

The routes are designed to stay away from busy main roads as much as possible and to allow cyclists to discover the peaceful back lanes, coastal tracks, bridleways and cycleways that cross this area, passing all manner of museums, castles, historic houses and other attractions. Although the major roads are busy, particularly in summer, the back lanes have remarkably little traffic. The areas covered by these routes are still predominantly rural – many of the towns and villages have preserved their traditional character which you will see along the way.

Some of the routes use sections of the West Country Way, part of the National Cycle Network, which is being developed by the charity Sustrans, with the help of a £43.5 million grant from the Millennium Commission. The cycle network will run through towns and cities and link urban areas with the countryside. The West Country Way will run from Padstow, through Bude and Barnstaple, over Exmoor to Tiverton and on to Bristol and Bath. For further information on the National Cycle Network write to Sustrans, 35 King Street, Bristol, BS1 4DZ, telephone (0117) 926 8893, or visit their web site at www.sustrans.org.uk.

There are hilly sections to be tackled in some of the routes – both inland and on the coast. However, this is compensated for by the spectacular views – and you can always get off and push your bike!

Geology, geography and history

Cornwall and Devon together comprise the south west peninsula of mainland Britain. Most of Cornwall is formed from Devonian strata, created millions of years ago, and a spine of granite, cut by deep river estuaries. Devon is famous for the red sandstone around Exeter, but to the east are found plateaux of Cretaceous Greensands, to the south chalky cliffs, limestone, shale and slate, to the north carboniferous rocks, and across Dartmoor the hard granite that has formed the prominent tors.

Cornwall has been occupied since before the Celtic Iron Age people settled here, around 700BC. The Romans made little impact and after their departure Cornwall became part of the Celtic kingdom of Dumnonia. Cornwall was briefly held by the Saxons before the Normans conquered and founded the first towns. The Cornish were fiercely independent, retaining their separate language until the English Book of Common Prayer was introduced in 1549 and the Cornish language died out. Well-known for their

Typical Devon thatch

seamanship, the Cornish helped defeat the Spanish Armada and piracy often helped supplement the local economy. Tin has been mined since the earliest times but in the 18th century copper mining became Cornwall's largest industry. When the market for Cornish copper failed, tin mining was revived but, by the late 19th century, most of Cornwall's mines were abandoned. Around the same time, the traditional fishing industry also suffered. The development of the railways brought some prosperity back to Cornwall – fresh fruit and vegetables were sent rapidly to market; and holiday makers started to visit the area, creating the tourist trade which is so important to the economy today.

Like Cornwall, Devon contains large numbers of prehistoric and ancient monuments. Devon was held by the Celtic Dumnonii tribe before the Romans conquered the area, building Exeter (Dumnoniorum). After the Romans withdrew, the Celts re-established themselves before being usurped by the Saxons. The Celts had always used the prehistoric ridgeways, but the Saxons created lanes, linking villages and marking field boundaries, many of which can still be seen today. The Norman Conquest made little impact, although the introduction of sheep and the woollen industry later brought much wealth. With the growth in trade, Devon, particularly Plymouth, became famous for ship building and seafaring. The naval base at Devonport, founded in the 17th century, was at one time the largest employer in the south west. Today the navy still has a presence, but the area's economy depends mainly on agriculture and tourism.

Preparing for a cycling trip

Basic maintenance

A cycle ride is an immense pleasure, particularly on a warm sunny day. Nothing is better than coasting along a country lane gazing over the countryside. Unfortunately, not every cycling day is as perfect as

this, and it is important to make sure that your bike is in good order and that you are taking the necessary clothing and supplies with you.

Before you go out on your bicycle check that everything is in order. Pump the tyres up if needed, and check that the brakes are working properly and that nothing is loose – the brakes are the only means of stopping quickly and safely. If there is a problem and you are not sure that you can fix it, take the bike to a cycle repair shop – they can often deal with small repairs very quickly.

When you go out cycling it is important to take either a puncture repair kit or a spare inner tube – it is often quicker to replace the inner tube in the event of a puncture, though it may be a good idea to practise first. You also need a pump, and with a slow puncture the pump may be enough to get you home. To remove the tyre you need a set of tyre levers. Other basic tools are an Allen key and a spanner. Some wheels on modern bikes can be removed by quick release levers built into the bike. Take a lock for your bike and if you have to leave it at any time, leave it in public view and locked through the frame and front wheel to something secure.

What to wear and take with you

It is not necessary to buy specialised cycling clothes. If it is not warm enough to wear shorts wear trousers which are easy to move in but fairly close to the leg below the knee – leggings are ideal – as this stops the trousers catching the chain. If you haven't got narrow-legged trousers, bicycle clips will hold them in. Jeans are not a good idea as they are rather tight and difficult to cycle in, and if they get wet they take a long time to dry. If your shorts or trousers are thin you might get a bit sore from being too long on the saddle. This problem can be reduced by using a gel saddle, and by wearing thicker, or extra, pants. Once you are a committed cyclist you can buy cycling shorts; or undershorts which have a protective pad built in and which can be worn under anything. It is a good idea to wear several thin layers of clothes so that you can add or remove layers as necessary. A zip-fronted top gives easy temperature control. Make sure you have something warm and something waterproof.

If you wear shoes with a firm, flat sole you will be able to exert pressure on the pedals easily, and will have less work to do to make the bicycle move. Gloves not only keep your hands warm but protect them in the event that you come off, and cycling mittens which cushion your hands are not expensive. A helmet is not a legal requirement, but it will protect your head if you fall.

In general it is a good idea to wear bright clothing so that you can be easily seen by motorists, and this is particularly important when it is overcast or getting dark. If you might be out in the dark or twilight fit your bicycle with lights – by law your bicycle must have a reflector. You can also buy reflective bands for your ankles, or to wear over your shoulder and back, and these help motorists to see you.

You may be surprised how quickly you use up energy when cycling, and it is important to eat a carbohydrate meal before you set out. When planning a long ride, eat well the night before. You should eat small amounts of food regularly while you are cycling, or you may find that your energy suddenly disappears, particularly if there are hills or if the weather is cold. It is important to always carry something to eat with you – chocolate, bananas, biscuits – so that if you do start fading away you can restore yourself quickly. In warm weather you will sweat and use up fluid, and you always need to carry something to drink – water will do! Many bicycles have a fitment in which to put a water bottle, and if you don't have one a cycle shop should be able to fit one.

It is also a good idea to carry a small first aid kit. This should include elastoplasts or bandages,

sunburn cream, and an anti-histamine in case you are stung by a passing insect.

It is a good idea to have a pannier to carry all these items. Some fit on the handlebars, some to the back of the seat and some onto a back rack. For a day's ride you probably won't need a lot of carrying capacity, but it is better to carry items in a pannier rather than in a rucksack on your back. Pack items that you are carrying carefully – loose items can be dangerous.

Getting to the start of the ride

If you are lucky you will be able to cycle to the start of the ride, but often transport is necessary. If you travel there by train, some sprinter services carry two bicycles without prior booking. Other services carry bicycles free in off-peak periods, but check the details with your local station. Alternatively, you could use your car – it may be possible to get a bike in the back of a hatchback if you take out the front wheel. There are inexpensive, easily fitted car racks which carry bicycles safely. Your local cycle store will be able to supply one to suit you.

Cycling on-road

Cycling on back roads is a delight with quiet lanes, interesting villages, good views and a smooth easy surface to coast along on. The cycle rides in this book are mainly on quiet roads but you sometimes cross busy roads or have stretches on B roads, and whatever sort of road you are on it is essential to ride safely. Always be aware of the possibility or existence of other traffic. Glance behind regularly, signal before you turn or change lane, and keep to the left. If there are motorists around, make sure that they have seen you before you cross their path. Cycling can be dangerous if you are competing for space with motor vehicles, many of which seem to have difficulty in seeing cyclists. When drivers are coming out of side

Land's End

roads, catch their eye before you ride in front of them.

You will find that many roads have potholes and uneven edges. They are much more difficult to spot when you are in a group because of the restricted view ahead, and therefore warnings need to be given. It is a good idea to cycle about a metre out into the road, conditions permitting, so that you avoid the worst of the uneven surfaces and to give you room to move in to the left if you are closely overtaken by a motor vehicle.

Other things to be careful of are slippery roads, particularly where there is mud or fallen leaves. Sudden rain after a period of dry weather often makes the roads extremely slippery. Dogs, too, are a hazard because they often move unpredictably, and sometimes like to chase cyclists. If you are not happy, stop or go slowly until the problem has passed.

Pedalling

Many modern bikes have 18 or 21 gears with three rings at the front and six or seven on the back wheel, and for much of the time you will find that the middle gear at the front with the range of gears at the back will be fine. Use your gears to find one that is easy to pedal along in so that your feet move round easily and you do not put too much pressure on your knees. If you are new to the bike and the gears it is a good idea to practise changing the gears on a stretch of flat, quiet road so that when you need to change gears quickly you will be ready to do so.

Cycling in a group

When cycling in a group it is essential to do so in a disciplined manner for your own, and others', safety. Do not ride too close to the bicycle in front of you – keep about a bicycle's length between you so that you will have space to brake or stop. Always keep both hands on the handlebars, except when signalling, etc. It is alright to cycle two abreast on quiet roads, but if it is necessary to change from cycling two abreast to single file this is usually done by the outside rider falling in behind the nearside rider; always cycle in single file where there are double white lines, on busy roads, or on narrow and winding roads where you have a restricted view of the road ahead. Overtake on the right (outside) only; do not overtake on the inside.

It is important to pass information to other members of the group, for example:

car up – a vehicle is coming up behind the group and will be overtaking;

car down – a vehicle is coming towards the group;

single up – get into single file;

stopping – stopping, or

slowing/easy – slowing due to junction, etc., ahead;

on the left – there is an obstacle on the left, e.g. pedestrian, parked car;

pothole – pothole (and point towards it).

Accidents

In case of an accident, stay calm and, if needed, ring the emergency services on 999. It is a good idea to carry a basic first aid kit and perhaps also one of the commercial foil wraps to put around anyone who has an accident to keep them warm. If someone comes off their bicycle move them and the bike off the road if it is safe to do so. Get someone in the party to warn approaching traffic to slow down, and if necessary ring for an ambulance.

Cycling off-road

All the routes in this book take you along legal rights of way – bridleways, byways open to all traffic and roads used as public paths – it is illegal to cycle along footpaths. Generally the off-road sections of the routes will be easy if the weather and ground are dry. If the weather has been wet and the ground is muddy, it is not a good idea to cycle along bridleways unless you do not mind getting dirty and unless you have a mountain bike which will not get blocked up with mud. In dry weather any bicycle will be able to cover the bridleway sections, but you may need to dismount if the path is very uneven.

Off-road cycling is different to cycling on the road. The average speed is lower, you will use more energy, your riding style will be different and there is a different set of rules to obey – the off-road code:

1 Give way to horse riders and pedestrians, and use a bell or call out to warn someone of your presence.

2 Take your rubbish with you.

3 Do not light fires.

4 Close gates behind you.

5 Do not interfere with wildlife, plants or trees.

6 Use only tracks where you have a right of way, or where the landowner has given you permission to ride.

7 Avoid back wheel skids, which can start erosion gulleys and ruin the bridleway.

Some of the off-road rides take you some miles from shelter and civilisation – take waterproofs, plenty of food and drink and basic tools – especially spare inner tubes and tyre repair equipment. Tell someone where you are going and approximately when you are due back. You are more likely to tumble off your bike riding off-road, so you should consider wearing a helmet and mittens with padded palms.

Local Tourist Information Centres

Cornwall

Cornwall Tourist Board
Daniell Road Centre, Truro
Telephone (01872) 274057

Bodmin
Mount Folly Square, Bodmin
Telephone (01208) 76616

Bude
The Cresent, Bude
Telephone (01288) 354240

Holsworthy
Manor Car Park, Holsworthy
Telephone (01409) 254185

Launceston
The Arcade, Launceston
Telephone (01566) 772321

Looe
The Guildhall, Fore Street, Looe
Telephone (01503) 262072

Padstow
North Quay, Padstow
Telephone (01841) 533449

Penzance
Station Approach, Penzance
Telephone (01736) 796297

Perranporth
Sainairs Arms, Perranporth
Telephone (01872) 573368

Devon

Devon Tourist Board
Exeter Motorway Services (M5)
Sidmouth Road, Exeter
Telephone (01392) 437581

Barnstaple
36 Boutport Street, Barnstaple
Telephone (01271) 75000

Holsworthy
Manor Car Park, Holsworthy
Telephone (01409) 254185

Honiton
Lace Walk, Honiton
Telephone (01404) 43716

Kingsbridge
The Quay, Kingsbridge
Telephone (01548) 853195

Lynton
Town Hall, Lynton
Telephone (01598) 752225

Okehampton
Museum Courtyard, West Street, Okehampton
Telephone (01837) 53020

Plymouth
The Barbican, Plymouth
Telephone (01752) 264849

Tiverton
Phoenix Lane, Tiverton
Telephone (01884) 255827

Local cycle hire

Cornwall

Bike Chain
Redruth
Telephone (01209) 215270

Bridge Bike Hire
The Camel Trail, Wadebridge
Telephone (01208) 813050

R.C. Pender
Jennings Street, Penzance
Telephone (01736) 332727

Devon

Bideford Bicycle Hire
Torrington Street, East the Water, Bideford
Telephone (01237) 424123

Burrator Bicycles
Peek Hill Farm, Dousland
Telephone (01822) 852908

Okehampton Cycle Centre
Bostock Garden Centre, North Road, Okehampton
Telephone (01837) 53248

Tarka Trail Cycle Hire
British Rail Station, Barnstaple
Telephone (01271) 24202

Torrington Cycle Hire
Unit 1, Station Yard, Torrington
Telephone (01805) 622633

Also Cycle Honiton and Tavistock Cycles (see below).

Local cycle shops

Cornwall

Bikebitz
Albert Street, Penzance
Telephone (01736) 333243

Devon

Cycle Honiton
King Street, Honiton
Telephone (01404) 47211

Saddles & Paddles
The Quay, Exeter
Telephone (01392) 424241

Tavistock Cycles Ltd
Paddons Row, Brook Street, Tavistock
Telephone (01822) 617630

WADEBRIDGE, PADSTOW AND THE CAMEL TRAIL

Route information

Distance 18.5km (11.5 miles) or 26.5km (16.5 miles)

Grade Easy

Terrain Well-surfaced, flat cycle trail. The optional extension to this route is on quiet lanes and a short section of B road.

Time to allow 2–3 hours.

Getting there by car Wadebridge is reached via the A39 or A389. There is car parking at Bridge Bike Hire (nominal charge, and refundable if hiring bikes). Bridge Bike Hire and the Camel Trail are signposted from Wadebridge.

Getting there by train There is no practical railway access to this ride.

This route starts from Wadebridge and follows the Camel Trail, a track on a disused railway, to Padstow. You can either return back along the Camel Trail or extend the route by 8km (5 miles) by taking the ferry from Padstow across the River Camel, and cycling back to Wadebridge on the northern side of the Camel estuary. A little care should be taken between directions 9 and 10 due to traffic, but the ride is quiet and the views pleasant. For details of the ferry (which runs all year), telephone Wadebridge Tourist Information Centre, number below.

Places of interest along the route

A Wadebridge

Wadebridge is an ancient port and market town. The birth of the town as a major trading centre came in 1460 when the Vicar of St Petroc built Wadebridge's famous 17-arched bridge, linking the north and south sides of the Camel estuary. The local name for the bridge is Bridge on Wool, and today it is unclear whether this refers to the fact that the construction was paid for by wealthy wool merchants, or as local legend says, that the bridge piers are sunk on woolsacks. The River Camel and Camel estuary were great sources of inspiration for the Poet Laureate, Sir John Betjeman, who is buried in nearby St Enodoc churchyard at Rock. The **John Betjeman Centre** in Wadebridge has a memorabilia room, containing Betjeman's desk, chair, drafts of his books and other objects. Opening times vary – telephone (01208) 812392 for further information. For further information on Wadebridge, telephone the Tourist Information Centre on (01208) 813725.

B Camel Trail

The Camel Trail is a 27km (17 mile) stretch of traffic free path and part of the National Cycle Network. It runs between Padstow and the source of the River Camel, on the edge of Bodmin Moor. The trail follows the route of the Atlantic Coast Express, a railway line opened in the late 19th century, linking Padstow and London Waterloo. The line carried thousands of holiday-makers to the West Country, until its closure in 1967. There is a lot of wildlife along the trail at all times of year, from otter, to salmon, kingfisher and heron. Seats are placed at intervals and there are plenty of good picnic spots. Open at all times, access free. Cornwall County Council maintain the trail and there are honesty boxes along the route – donations towards the continued existence and upkeep of the trail are appreciated. For further information telephone Cornwall County Council on (01208) 815631.

⒞ Padstow

A delightful town situated around a harbour. Numerous ice cream and gift shops and crazy golf overlooking the sea. Medieval buildings are still visible in the old quarter of the town and around the old port, originally named after St Petroc, an Irish missionary who landed at Padstow in the 6th century. Padstow has been made famous by Rick Stein and his TV series on seafood – his seafood restaurant is in the town. Telephone the Tourist Information Centre for further information on (01841) 533449. The **Padstow Museum** illustrates the history of the town with many interesting artefacts and photographs. Open Easter to October, Monday–Friday 1000–1230 and 1400–1700, Saturday 1000–1230. Nominal charge. Telephone the Tourist Information Centre for further information.

⒟ Prideaux Place, Padstow

Prideaux Place is an Elizabethan mansion, built in the 1580s by the Prideaux-Brune family. The house comprises 81 rooms, 44 of which are bedrooms, although only six are habitable – many of the bedrooms are just as they were left by the American Army at the end of the Second World War. However, there are grand rooms open to the public. The house has been much used as a film location and there is an exhibition of past film work. Tours of the house, also deer park, formal gardens, restored stables and tearoom. Open Easter to October, Sunday–Thursday 1330–1700. Charge. Telephone (01841) 532411 for further information.

Padstow, on the Camel Estuary

Food and drink

There is lots of choice in Wadebridge and Padstow, and a post office and stores in Chapel Amble.

Mulsters Arms, Chapel Amble
Cream teas served 1500–1700 during the summer.

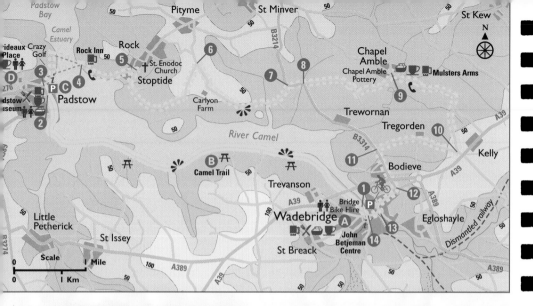

Route description

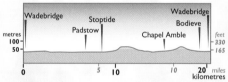

TR out of the Bridge Bike Hire car park and follow SP to the Camel Trail, 200m away.

1 Cycle along the Camel Trail, towards Padstow, passing several old quarries, with views of the Camel estuary to the right.

2 To visit Padstow or cycle the extended route SO at the end of the trail (8.5km/5 miles). Pass seats on left and cycle through car park towards old station (metal bike stands here). Enter the one way system and cycle along the quay.

3 To visit Prideaux Place, TL into Duke Street, continue SO into Fentonluna Lane and then TR into Tregiris Lane. Prideaux Place is on the left. Otherwise TR, no SP, following the edge of the quay (Tourist Information Centre on right). The road splits – RHF goes to ferry at most times (clearly marked by a flag and green board). To catch ferry at low tide, take LHF up hill, past crazy golf.

4 From slipway on other side of estuary, TR, no SP, and pass the Rock Inn on the left. Continue into Rock.

5 TR, SP Trehilly (10.5km/6.5 miles), and descend, staying on this road.

6 TR, no SP (13.5km/8.5 miles). Head towards tower and pass Carlyon Farm on right. Excellent views right along estuary. The road descends (20% gradient).

7 TR at TJ, SP Wadebridge. *16km (10 miles)*

8 TL, SP Chapel Amble and continue into village.

9 TR at TJ opposite Chapel Amble pottery, SP Wadebridge (19km/12 miles). Continue out of village.

10 TR, no SP (22.5km/14 miles). Pass Tregorden on the right.

11 TL at TJ onto B3314, SP Wadebridge.

12 TR at TJ (roundabout), SP Wadebridge. Continue downhill on cycle path, along side of road.

13 TR at roundabout, SP Padstow/St Columb/Newquay/Truro. Cross bridge.

14 TR at TJ (roundabout), SP Truro. Continue back to Bridge Bike Hire to finish the route. *26.5km (16.5 miles)*

TOTNES AND THE SOUTH DEVON RAILWAY

Route information

 Distance 20km (12.5 miles)

 Grade Moderate

 Terrain Quiet lanes and three off-road sections – two on byways and the third on a traffic-free cycle track developed by Sustrans. There are a few short steep climbs.

Time to allow 2–3 hours.

Getting there by car Totnes is signed from the A380 Exeter to Torbay road. Take the A385 and follow SP for one of the several long stay car parks in the town.

Getting there by train Totnes is on the main line into the West Country. Telephone (0345) 484950 for timetable information.

From Totnes Station the route goes through the town before climbing out towards Berry Pomeroy. On past Berry Pomeroy Castle and, after a descent and a further climb, views of southern Dartmoor open out. Continue along a series of quiet lanes and onto a pair of byways. Both are downhill, and care should be taken on the second one to avoid a small drop into a water channel on the left. There is an optional on-road route, avoiding both byways. Past Staverton Railway, a privately-run steam railway on the South Devon Railway, and a short section of the A384 leads to the Totnes Cycleway, completing the route.

Places of interest along the route

A Totnes

Totnes sits on a hill overlooking the River Dart. The Saxons built earthworks on the hill which were replaced by the Normans during the 11th century. The Normans also built **Totnes Castle**, an English Heritage property. Gift shop; picnics welcome. Open April to October, daily 1000–1800 (or dusk if earlier); November to March, Wednesday–Sunday 1000–1600. Charge. Telephone (01803) 864406. The town is full of craft shops, book and antique shops, and visitors can take boat trips on the River Dart. Telephone the Tourist Information Centre for more information on (01803) 863168.

B Berry Pomeroy Castle, Berry Pomeroy

The estates at Berry Pomeroy have been owned by only two families since the Norman invasion. The castle was built by the Pomeroy family in the 14th century. In 1547 it was sold to Edward Seymour, Duke of Somerset. Today visitors can see the Pomeroys' gatehouse and the ruins of the Seymours' stone mansion. English Heritage property. Tearoom, picnics welcome. Open April to October, daily 1000–1800 (or dusk if earlier). Charge. Telephone (01392) 382800.

C South Devon Railway, Staverton Station

The South Devon Railway and its steam trains link Totnes with Buckfastleigh and Buckfast Abbey, via Staverton. The railway runs alongside the River Dart, through glorious scenery. The journey from Staverton to Buckfastleigh takes around ten minutes and there is a café, maze, railway museum, engine shed, butterfly and otter sanctuary, and Buckfast Abbey. Alternatively, you could catch the train back into Totnes (bicycles carried). Telephone (01364) 642338 for further information.

Near Totnes

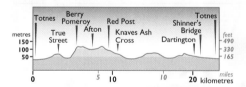

TL out of the station. Then, TL at TJ, SP Torquay/Painton/Brixham/Totnes Town Centre. Pass Devon Ceramics and Visitor Centre on right. Take third exit at roundabout, SP Town Centre. Pass Tourist Information Centre on left. At next roundabout TL, SP Boats/River Trips. Cross the river. Pass Parish Church on right. TR at TJ, SP Paignton. Climb, continuing along the A385.

1 TL, SP Berry Pomeroy/Berry Pomeroy Castle. Enter Berry Pomeroy.

2 SO at XR, SP Marldon/Castle/Torquay. Climb out of village.

3 TL, SP Berry Pomeroy Castle/Afton. Pass entrance to Berry Pomeroy Castle on left (4.5km/3 miles). The castle is 1km (0.6 mile) up the track. Otherwise, continue towards Afton. Climb a little further before a steep descent along a wooded lane. Bear left through the tiny hamlet of Afton, after which another climb leads to a flattish lane with lovely views of Dartmoor straight ahead.

4 SO at XR, SP Fishacre Barton/ Broadhempston, and descend.

5 TL at Knaves Ash Cross, SP Staverton (9km/5.5 miles). Descend, passing under a railway bridge. Follow road as it bends left and then right, following SP Staverton.

Food and drink

Totnes has lots of places for refreshment, and there is a tearoom at Berry Pomeroy Castle.

Red Post Garage, A381
Chocolate bars and drinks for sale.

Sea Trout Inn, Staverton
Traditional village inn. Bar meals available.

Cider Press Centre, Totnes
A large collection of gift shops and eateries under one roof, on the way back into Totnes. Often musicians and acrobats providing entertainment. A good place to stop.

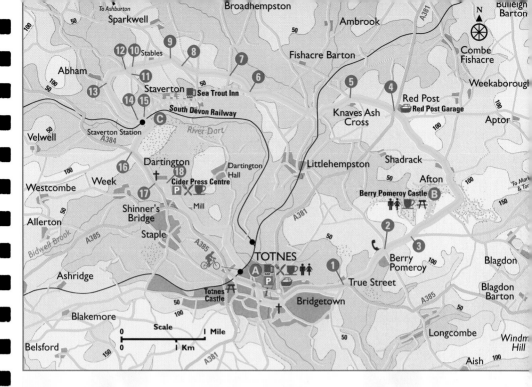

6 To avoid byways, SO at XR (Copper Tree Cross), following SP Staverton. Rejoin route at direction 15, where continue round left bend, SP Staverton Bridge. Otherwise, TR at XR, SP Landscove/Ashburton.

7 SO at XR (Waddons Cross), no SP.

8 TR at TJ (effectively SO). Cross SLOW sign on the road.

9 TL onto Public Byway. Pass stables on right. Continue downhill, along narrow but firm byway.

10 TL at TJ (effectively SO), no SP.

13.5km (8.5 miles)

11 TR, SP Bumpston/Buckfastleigh.

12 TL, SP Public Byway. The surface is firm but be careful to avoid a small drop into a water channel on left.

13 TL at TJ, no SP, back onto tarmac (14.5km/9 miles). Continue along a wooded valley floor.

14 TL at TJ (effectively SO), no SP. Pass Staverton Station on right.

15 TR at TJ, SP Staverton Bridge.

16 TL at TJ onto A384, SP Totnes. Take care on this short section of A road. You could walk along St Mary's Church footpath, on left after 200m. Just after church:

17 TL at XR, SP Dartington Hall.

18 TR onto Totnes Cycleway, indicated by a large green Sustrans route board. Follow track as it bends to the left around Cider Press Centre car park. Enter the centre, TL next to seats, pass toyshop and continue on the cycleway. Cycle along the path, round a mill on the left, and follow more Sustran green boards. At the fork – take LHF along smoother gravelled surface. At the road – TR at TJ, pass through gates and immediately TL back onto track. Keep on this track all the way back into Totnes, finishing at the station. *20km (12.5 miles)*

PERRANPORTH, ST AGNES AND PENHALLOW

Route information

Distance 21km (13 miles)

Grade Moderate

Terrain Tarmac surface throughout, on B and minor roads. Two climbs, one long and gradual, the other short and steep.

Time to allow 2–4 hours.

Getting there by car Perranporth is on the north coast of Cornwall, SP from the A30 Bodmin to Redruth road. There are two long stay car parks in the town: the one by the beach is cheaper but fills up quickly; the other car park is on the cliffs in the direction of the youth hostel.

Getting there by train There is no practical railway access to this ride.

Following a steady climb out of Perranporth, the route flattens before quickly descending into picturesque Trevellas Coombe. A steep climb takes you into the former mining town of St Agnes, from where the route follows more gentle contours through the rolling Cornish countryside. On to the village of Callestick, before heading back along minor roads to Perranporth

Route description

Start at the Tourist Information Centre, Perranporth, beside the beach. Cycle away from the beach and TR into St George's Road, SP St Agnes. Steady climb for 1.5km (1 mile), then road flattens out. Views of windmills to left, airfield to right. Continue on this road (B3285).

1 TR, SP Cross Coombe/Trevellas Porth.

2 TR, SP Cross Coombe.

3 TR, SP Cross Coombe. Descend into beautiful Trevellas Coombe. Pass Blue Hills Tin Streams on left, before hard (33% gradient) climb for 1km (0.6 mile).

4 TL just before Dead End SP and next to Wheal Kitty Workshops (5.5km/3.5 miles). Pass Seabreeze House on right.

5 TR at TJ, SP St Agnes/Truro, and descend into St Agnes. Pass the Saffron Gallery on the right. Bear left and climb up British Road. At top, bear left, SP Truro.

6 TL next to red post box and opposite the Railway Inn, no SP. Descend.

7 TR at TJ into Goonown Road, no SP. Continue on this road towards Goonbell.

8 TL, SP Wheal Batson/Silverwell. Gentle descent then short climb.

9 TL sharply, no SP (10km/6 miles). Former railway viaduct on left.

10 TR at TJ, no SP (TL crosses railway bridge).

11 TL at TJ, no SP (TR goes to Truro). Descend, crossing old railway bridge.

12 TR SP Perranporth/Truro. Descend, crossing weak bridge. Bear right, following SP Callestick.

13 SO at XR, SP Penhallow.

14 SO at XR, SP Callestick (14.5km/9 miles). Pass Callestock Cider Farm on right.

15 TL, SP Perran Church/Perranporth. Pass Callestick Farm on right.

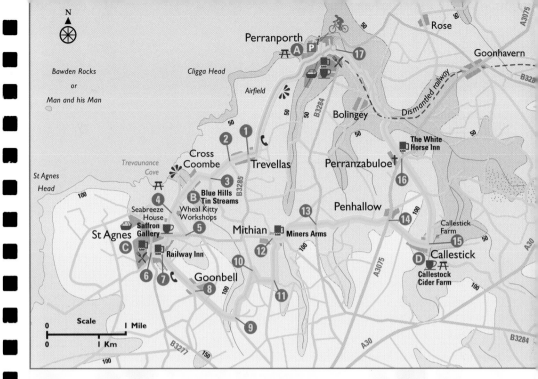

16 SO at XR (opposite church) to cross A3075. Follow this road back into Perranporth.

17 TL at roundabout, SP St Agnes and return to Tourist Information Centre and the end of the route. ***21km (13 miles)***

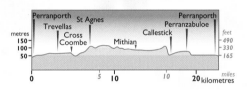

Food and drink

Plenty of choice in Perranporth and St Agnes. There is a tearoom at Callestock Cider Farm.

 Saffron Gallery, St Agnes
Tearooms located above gallery and gift shop.

 Miners Arms, Mithian
Bar meals served. Families welcome.

Places of interest along the route

A Perranporth

Perranporth, like many towns and villages in this area, was a mining community. However, all traces of its mining history have disappeared and Perranporth is now a popular holiday destination, well-known for its 4.5km (3 mile) stretch of beautiful sandy beach. For further information, telephone the Tourist Information Centre on (01872) 573368.

B Blue Hills Tin Streams, Trevellas Coombe

Tin has been produced here for thousands of

Stippy Stappy, St Agnes

years. The many small mines were incorporated into the Blue Hills Sett in the early 19th century, and over 100 men were employed here until its closure in 1897. Tin production, however, has never ceased and visitors can see how the ore is processed during a guided tour of the tin works. Giftshop selling items made of Cornish tin. The tour lasts approximately 1½ hours. Open April to October, Monday–Saturday 1030–1700; November to March, please telephone to confirm opening. Charge. Telephone (01872) 553341.

ⓒ St Agnes

St Agnes was also founded on tin mining and now promotes itself as a coastal resort. There are still the original miners' cottages and the much-photographed terrace of Stippy Stappy. A craft trail leads visitors around the village, to workshops and craft centres, ending at Trevaunance Cove. The cove contains the remains of a once busy harbour – constructed several times since the 18th century, the most recent harbour was destroyed in storms during 1915 and 1916. The area was used as a location during the filming of *Poldark* and, more recently, for the television detective series *Wycliffe*. Telephone St Agnes Tourist Information Centre for more information on (01872) 554150.

ⓓ Callestock Cider Farm

Over 40 varieties of jam, traditional farm scrumpy and many other food stuffs are produced here. Visitors can follow the cider-making process and see the jam kitchen. Also Cider Museum, trailer ride through the orchards and farm animals. Picnic area and tearooms serving morning coffee, lunch and cream teas. Open February to December, Monday–Friday 0900–1800; Easter to October also open Saturday 0900–1800; mid-June to mid-September also open Sunday 1000–1800; July and August, Monday–Saturday 0900–2000. Nominal charge for entrace to Cider Museum, otherwise free admission. Telephone (01872) 573356.

OKEHAMPTON AND DARTMOOR

Route information

Distance 22.5km (14 miles)

Grade Strenuous

Terrain A hard climb at the start, followed by a mostly tarmacked loop into Dartmoor, and two off-road sections that are not too testing.

Time to allow 2–4 hours.

Getting there by car Okehampton is signed from the A30, the main route into Cornwall. There are pay and display car parks in town. The most convenient car park is 100m from the Tourist Information Centre, in the centre of town.

Getting there by train Sunday service from Exeter during the summer. Telephone (01837) 55330 for information.

A beautiful route, providing wonderful views of Dartmoor, in a safe fashion. Starting from the Tourist Information Centre, a hard, steep climb takes you up on to Dartmoor. From here, the route follows a military ring road into the centre of the moor. Although tarmacked most of the way, there are a number of short sections of loose road. Having admired the extensive views across the moor and beyond, you descend on a stony track to the pretty village of Belstone. From here, the route follows a lovely bridleway, parallel to the East Okement River, back into Okehampton. A shorter circuit can be made, if you wish to avoid a lot of climbing.

Places of interest along the route

Ⓐ Okehampton

Okehampton is an ancient market town on the northern side of Dartmoor. The area was first settled during the Bronze Age. The Romans, Celts and Saxons followed, to be overthrown by the Normans, who built **Okehampton Castle**. The substantial ruins, now in the hands of English Heritage, comprise the largest Medieval castle in Devon. Audio tour, woodland trail, gift shop and riverside picnic area. Open April to October, daily 1000–1800 (or dusk if earlier). Charge. Telephone (01837) 52844. The **Museum of Dartmoor Life** tells the story of the people who have lived and worked on Dartmoor, from pre-historic times to the present day. Also on the site are tearooms, a jewellery studio, craft shop and the Tourist Information Centre. Open Easter to October, Monday–Saturday 1000–1700; June to September also open Sunday; November to March, Monday–Friday 1000–1600. Charge for entry to museum. Telephone the Tourist Information Centre on (01837) 52295. **Okehampton Railway Station** was originally opened in October 1871 and finally closed in June 1972. The station is undergoing restoration and a Sunday train service is run during the summer months. There is a model shop on site, as well as exhibition and video presentation, gift shop and model railway. The Bulleid Buffet is a licensed restaurant serving coffee, lunches, cream teas and dinners. Open June to September, Tuesday–Sunday and Bank Holidays 1000–1730; October to May, Wednesday–Sunday and Bank Holidays 1000–1700. Charge for entrance to exhibition and video presentation only. Telephone (01837) 55330.

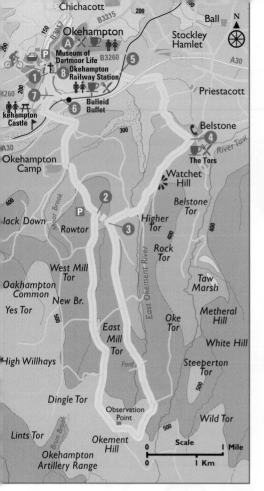

Route description

From the Tourist Information Centre, TR down West Street, then TR into George Street, SP Okehampton Camp.

1   TR into Station Road, SP Okehampton Camp/Walking Centre/Youth Hostel. Continue on this road as it becomes Tors Road. Pass golf club on right. Climb steeply, crossing the railway and the dual carriageway. Continue as the road flattens and Okehampton Camp appears on the right. Ignore the roads into the camp, cross a cattle grid and a ford (ignoring the track to the right), and keep climbing on the tarmac road.

2   To avoid military ring road, take LHF (4km/2.5 miles) just past car park, and continue route at direction 3, where TL onto stony track. Otherwise, just past car park, RHF (4km/2.5 miles), passing a one bar gate. Follow this loop road as it gradually climbs towards Okement Hill. The road is mostly sealed, though there are occasional short unsealed sections. At the observation point the road swings left and you descend. Pass through a ford.

3   This turn is easy to miss – just after crossing a small bridge, TR (14.5km/9 miles) onto stony track that descends to cross a pair of small stone bridges. Immediately after bridges, take LHF and cross Watchet Hill. Pass through a gate and back onto tarmac, descending into the small village of Belstone.

4   TL just before telephone box, no SP. Descend, passing plaster horses on edge of an orchard on right.

5   TL at TJ (Fatherford Bridge), no SP (20.5km/12.5 miles). Then, TL, SP Bridlepath to Fatherford/Station road/Klondyke Corner. Pass through gate, pass under viaduct, cross bridge and TR, SP Bridlepath Station Road. Continue along this well-surfaced path, through a valley. Pass entrance (steps) to Okehampton Station.

6   TR at TJ just below station entrance, no SP. Descend.

7   TR at TJ into Station Road, SP Town Centre.

8   TL at TJ opposite the church, into George Street, no SP. Then TL into West Street, to the Tourist Information Centre and the end of the route.   ***22.5km (14 miles)***

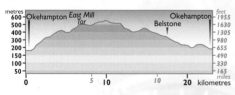

Food and drink

There is plenty of choice in Okehampton and refreshments are available at the Bulleid Buffet, Okehampton Station.

The Tors, Belstone
Morning coffee, lunch and dinner served.

Route information

Distance 23km (14.5 miles)

Grade Moderate

Terrain Mostly quiet roads, with a section of private and B road. One short steep climb.

Time to allow 2–3 hours.

Getting there by car Gweek is on the Helford River, at the top of the Lizard Peninsula. Take the A3083 from Helston to the Lizard, and then, just after RNAS Culdrose, the B3293. Gweek is SP from this road. There is car parking in the village and at the National Seal Sanctuary.

Getting there by train There is no practical railway access to this ride.

Starting from the National Seal Sanctuary in Gweek, a steady but gentle climb through woodland takes you to Trelowarren estate. From here the route heads south along quiet roads to the B3293, before turning north, across Goonhilly Downs, to RNAS Culdrose. A lovely descent takes you back to Gweek.

Places of interest along the route

Ⓐ National Seal Sanctuary, Gweek

The National Seal Sanctuary is located on the upper reaches of the Helford estuary and has been operating for 40 years. The sanctuary is one of Europe's major marine animal rescue centres, rescuing, rehabilitating and releasing around 30 sick, injured or abandoned seal pups each year. Visitors can see the seals and sealions and watch feeding demonstrations. Also audio-visual presentation, underwater observatory, woodland walks and landscaped gardens. Gift shop, café, barbecue, picnic and children's play area. Open all year, 0900–1700 (1600 in winter). Charge. Telephone (01326) 221874.

Ⓑ Haliggye Fogou, Trelowarren

An underground gallery with subsidiary passages constructed of drystone walling. It was occupied between the late Iron Age and Roman times. Historians are unsure as to whether it was a cellar, refuge or ritual centre. Take a torch, as it is dark inside. Located about 400m from the road, on the Trelowarren estate. Open at all reasonable times. Admission free.

Ⓒ Trelowarren

The Trelowarren estate has been owned by the same family since 1427. Occupied by the army during the Second World War, the house and grounds are now undergoing restoration. There is plenty to see and do. The Lizard Countryside Centre introduces visitors to the Lizard Peninsula, its people, landscape, flora and fauna, through photography, touch screen computers and computer imaging. Open Easter to September, daily 1100–1700. Admission free. Telephone (01326) 221661. Waymarked woodland walks cross the estate, visiting the quay and Haliggye Fogou. Picnics welcome. The gardens at Trelowarren were developed during the 18th century and are being rebuilt and restored to the original design. Walks and gardens open Easter to September, daily 1100–1700. Admission free. Tours of the house are offered Easter to September, Wednesdays and Bank Holiday Mondays, 1415–1700. Charge. Telephone (01326) 221366. The Cornwall Crafts Association has a gallery with a permanent display of Cornish crafts and an annual programme of changing exhibitions. Pottery and weaving studio. Open Easter to September, telephone (01326) 221567 to confirm times. Also Yard Restaurant serving coffee, lunches and evening meals.

D Goonhilly Nature Reserve, Goonhilly Downs

A soil of serpentine rock and a mild maritime climate support a wide variety of habitats, home to many wild creatures. This is the hunting ground of Hen Harriers and Short Eared Owls. There are Cornish heath flowers in the late summer – the controlled burning and grazing by Exmoor ponies allow smaller plants to flower.

E Earth Station Goonhilly, Goonhilly Downs

The largest satellite station on earth. Visitor centre, multi media command centre and internet zone. Also restaurant and children's play area. Open April to November, daily 1000–1700. Charge. Telephone 0800 679593.

F RNAS Culdrose, near Helston

The largest helicopter base in Europe. Viewing station from where visitors can watch the daily activities and see several static aircraft displays. Tearoom and gift shop. Open all year, daily 1000–1700. Admission free. Telephone Helston Tourist Information Centre for further information on (01326) 565431.

Route description

Leave the car park at the National Seal Sanctuary, TL at TJ, no SP, and cycle downhill. TL at TJ next to telephone box, cross a bridge and pass Gweek Quay on the left.

1 TL, SP Mawgan/Goonhilly Downs/St Keverne/Coverack, for a steady, gentle climb through woods.

2 SO at XR (roundabout), SP St Keverne/Coverack.

3 TL, SP Trelowarren, then TL at TJ (effectively SO) and TR through gates. Continue along the private road into Trelowarren, passing Haliggye Fogou on the right. Cross a cattle grid into the Trelowarren Estate. Visit the estate by going through pillars in front of you, or continue the route and bear right in front of the pillars. *6.5km (4 miles)*

4 TL, SP All Traffic.

5 TL at TJ back onto public roads, SP Helford/Manaccan.

6 TR, SP Tretharrup/Trelaminney (homemade SP). *10km (6 miles)*

7 TR, SP St Keverne/the Lizard.

8 TR at TJ (broken SP), then TR at TJ onto B3293, SP Helston. Take care on this road, although visibility for traffic is excellent. Pass Goonhilly Nature Reserve, and then Earth Station Goonhilly (14.5km/9 miles). Continue on this road.

Food and drink

Gweek has a pub, tearoom, licensed restaurant (with garden seating) and a convenience store. Refreshments are also available at the

National Seal Sanctuary, Trelowarren, Earth Station Goonhilly and RNAS Culdrose.

Goonhilly Craft Centre, Goonhilly Downs
Tearoom, craft centre, pottery and gift shop. Seating inside and out.

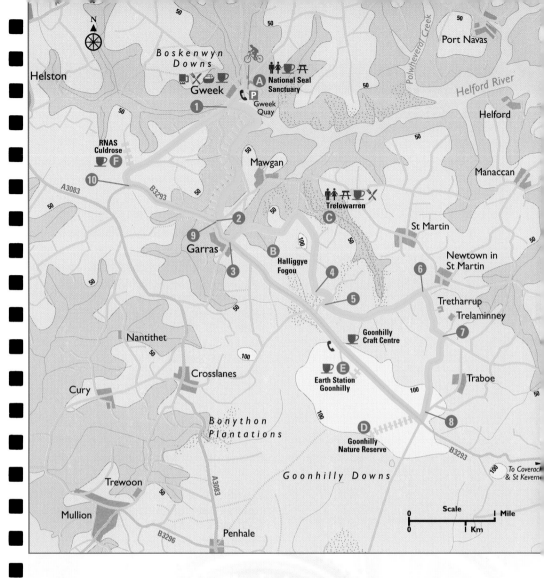

9 To avoid a climb (missing RNAS Culdrose) SO and return to Gweek. Otherwise, TL at XR (roundabout), SP Falmouth/Helston/Lizard.

10 TR SP Gweek. TL for RNAS Culdrose (20km/12.5 miles). Descend into Gweek and return to the National Seal Sanctuary and the end of the route.   ***23km (14.5 miles)***

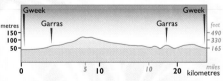

REDRUTH AND THE MINERAL TRAMWAYS

Route information

Distance 25.5km (16 miles)

Grade Moderate

Terrain Quiet lanes and good quality tracks.

Time to allow 2–4 hours.

Getting there by car Redruth is on the A30 Truro to Penzance road. There are several long term car parks close to Redruth Railway Station.

Getting there by train Redruth is on the main line through Cornwall. Telephone (0345) 484950 for information.

This route takes you through what was once the industrial heart of Cornwall, where, during the 18th and 19th centuries, massive deposits of tin and copper ore were mined. The countryside is littered with the remains of engine houses, mines and shafts. The route uses much of the Mineral Tramways, traffic-free tracks developed along the routes of the old tramways which were used to transport material between the mines, and to and from the sea ports. From Redruth, the route initially heads west onto a track (part of the Mineral Tramways project) before continuing along well-graded tracks and lanes, past numerous old engine houses, to enter the village of Carnkie. Quiet lanes take you through Carharrack and beyond, to an off-road descent to the edge of Twelveheads. A final section of off-road, criss-crossed with paths, leads through more mining sites, where the only sign of shafts are

the conical cages covering them. There are several parallel tracks here, so do not worry if you should miss a turn – keep cycling straight ahead and you will find the road leading to St Day, the final village before the return to Redruth.

Route description

Start at the entrance to Redruth Railway Station. Descend hill and take RHF at traffic lights just before bridge, SP RNAS Culdrose. Descend and TL at TJ (traffic lights), SP Falmouth/Helston. Pass under railway viaduct to TR into Trewirgie Road, and continue on this road as it turns into West Trewirgie Road. TL at TJ into Trevingey Road and descend to SO at XR, passing SP Dead End and a house called Just-A-Nic on the right. Ride along bridleway, admiring Carn Brea on left.

1 TL next to SP All Tipping Prohibited, passing between boulders. Continue along a narrower track, heading for and passing a five-ringed chimney.

2 SO at tarmac, pass the Cottage (house name) and bear right. Follow this road to TL at TJ, SP Great Flat Lode. Pass the Mineral Tramways Discovery Centre on the right.

4km (2.5 miles)

3 SO at XR, SP Carn Brea Leisure Centre. Then TL, SP Brea.

4 Just before road bears right, TL through a gate, onto gravel path. Follow this track as it climbs gently.

5 TR at TJ, SP Great Flat Lode, and back on to tarmac. TL at TJ, no SP. *5.5km (3.5 miles)*

6 TL next to two almost complete engine houses, no SP.

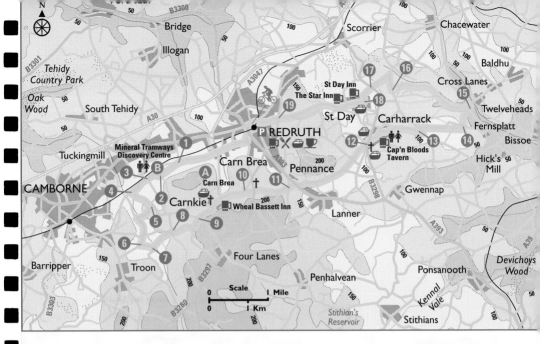

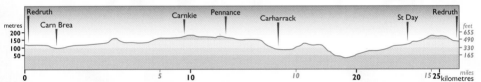

7 TL opposite a black galvanised shed, SP Great Flat Lode. Pass a single boulder and continue onto a flat track. TL when reach tarmac. Pass houses and TR at TJ (effectively SO).

8 TR on to Great Flat Lode (track). Pass between two large buildings and bear right, back onto tarmac. Almost immediately, TL at TJ, no SP.

9 SO at XR, no SP (opposite SP for Wheal Bassett Pub). Enter village. TR at TJ, opposite Methodist Church, no SP (9km/5.5 miles). Continue out of village and climb.

10 TR, SP Great Flat Lode (black arrow). Then, SO at XR by converted Wesleyan Chapel, no SP, onto bridleway.

11 SO at XR by radio masts, no SP. TR at

TJ, SP Falmouth. TL into Pennance Road. Continue downhill.

12 TL at TJ, SP Truro/St Day. TR by church, into Church Row. TR into United Road.
14.5 km (9 miles)

13 TL at TJ, SP Chasewater/Truro. Then TR, SP Fernsplatt/Hick's Mill/Bissoe. SO onto bridleway, as road bears left. SO at XR of bridleways, pass a house on right and take next TL descending to:

14 SO at XR. Cross tarmac on to another bridleway to descend further. When road is reached:

15 TL onto a bridleway along Poldice Valley. Pass Wheal Fortune Farm on left. Take LHF, SP Portreath, then LHF and short climb. Cycle for just under 1km (0.6 mile) and take RHF, following a green arrow. Continue and SO,

SP Portreath. Follow this upper track to a TJ of tracks where TL up a short climb (heading for old buildings). Bear right in front of these to follow track on the level as it passes between two wired fences, past houses on left.

16 TR at TJ, then TL at TJ, SP St Day/Carharrack. Climb. **21km (13 miles)**

17 SO at XR, SP St Day, and into village.

18 TR into Fore Street. Leave the village. Climb then descend to:

19 SO at XR (double roundabouts), SP Redruth. Descend to the station and the end of the route. **25.5km (16 miles)**

Food and drink

There are lots of places for refreshment in Redruth, pubs in Carnkie and Carharrack, and convenience stores in Carnkie, Carharrack and St Day.

St Day Inn, St Day
Basic pub food.

The Star Inn, St Day
Bar meals available.

Places of interest along the route

A Carn Brea

The first section of the route is overshadowed by Carn Brea, the site of an early Neolithic settlement, 226m (740 feet) high. On top of Carn Brea is a monument to Francis Bassett, a philanthropic 18th-century mine owner who worked to improve the living and working conditions of the mine labourers. Also on the hill are the remains of a Medieval construction, now a restaurant.

B Mineral Tramways Discovery Centre, near Redruth

The Mineral Tramways project is working to conserve the mining heritage of Cornwall's central mining district – through conservation work and by opening up the mineral tramways that served the mines. The centre contains exhibits describing the project and the work completed to date, and gives the history of the tramways themselves. Also shop selling local crafts, books and maps. Open all year, Tuesday–Friday 1000–1600, Saturday 1300–1600. Admission free. Telephone (01209) 612917 for further information.

Old tin mine

Route information

 Distance 26km (16 miles)

Grade Strenuous

Terrain Four sections of off-road riding make this a ride for a mountain bike. Otherwise, quiet lanes and a quiet B road.

Time to allow 2–4 hours.

Getting there by car Clovelly is on the north Devon coast, signed from the A39 Bideford to Bude road. Car parking (charge) is available next to the visitor centre.

Getting there by train There is no practical railway access to this ride.

Starting from Clovelly village, the route follows a mostly well-surfaced bridleway towards the sea, passing the National Trust Brownsham Nature Reserve and Hartland Point. A few miles of quiet lane take you onto a coastal bridleway, with stunning views of the coast and Lundy Island. The bridleway is a little demanding at times, but take your time and perhaps walk a section or two. The route then follows lanes to Hartland Point before two further bridleways take you to the village of Stoke. A quiet undulating B road takes you back into Clovelly.

Places of interest along the route

Ⓐ Clovelly

This picturesque village clings to a steep hillside. Cottages line the stepped, cobbled street – you will have to leave your bicycle at the Visitor Centre but there is landrover transport between the top of the village and the harbour (Easter to October). The Clovelly Centre/Tourist Information Centre has a tearoom, picnic area, gift shop and children's playground. In the village is a 19th-century fisherman's cottage, a Charles Kingsley exhibition, lifeboat museum and boat trips to Lundy Island. Tourist Information Centre and attractions open daily, all year, 1000–1700. Charge for parking and audio-visual presentation, fisherman's cottage, Kingsley exhibition and boat trips. Telephone (01237) 431781.

Ⓑ Clovelly Court Garden, Clovelly

Just outside the village, this garden is a classic example of a Victorian kitchen garden. Open April to September, daily 1000–1600. Charge. Telephone (01237) 431781.

Ⓒ Hartland Abbey, Hartland

A family home since 1539, the original abbey was founded circa 1157 and dissolved by Henry VIII in 1539. The house contains Queen Anne, Georgian, Regency and Victorian decoration. Also gardens and woodland walks. Tearoom. Open Easter and May to September, Wednesday, Thursday, Sunday and Bank Holidays (also Tuesday in July and August), 1400–1730. Charge. Telephone (01237) 441264.

Ⓓ The Milky Way, near Clovelly

Family adventure park with birds of prey, farm animals, and assault courses designed for adults and children. Tearoom. Open April to October, daily 1030–1800; November to March, weekends 1030–1800. Charge. Telephone (01237) 431255.

Clovelly

Route description

Exit the car park at the Clovelly Centre, going downhill. TL at the first TJ, no SP, and cycle along the road you drove in on.

1 TR as road bends to left, no SP.

2 To visit Clovelly Court Gardens, take road on right, no SP. Otherwise, take road on left between pillars and descend, SP Court Farm/Sawmills. Cycle through Court Farm and join bridleway, SP Bridleway on post on right. Follow track to left hand corner of field, then follow alongside hedge to gate. Pass through gate and down steep, rocky track.

3 TL at TJ, SP Public Bridleway. TR 200m later, at another SP Bridleway, and follow this well-surfaced track uphill. Pass entrance to Brownsham Nature Reserve on left and Lower Brownsham Farm on right.   *4km (2.5 miles)*

4 TL onto tarmac opposite farm, SP Lower Browsham Farm. Pass Brownsham Car Park on right.

5 TR at XR, SP Beckland/Exmansworthy/Fattacott.

6 TR, SP Exmansworthy/Fattacott/No Through Road (6.5km/4 miles). At end of road, pass through farm, SP Bridleway, and through gate onto a short track. At this point the path seems to disappear – continue through gate in corner of field and cycle along right side of hedge. At far corner climb stile (you are still on bridleway). The bridleway follows close to the cliffs, with the sea to the right (it is safe!), crossing several stiles. After 1.5km/1 mile the only way ahead is through a gate in top left corner of field. Go through this onto a track and immediately TR through another gate signed by a blue arrow. Pass through another field and onto a track that descends to join the coastal path (signed as such). After 300m there is a seat on right, where TL, SP East Titchberry Car Park.

7 TR at TJ, no SP (10.5km/6.5 miles). Pass National Trust car park on right, and later ticket booth for Hartland Point.

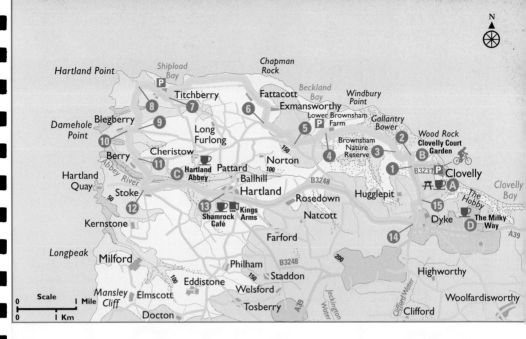

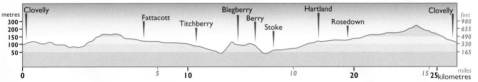

8 TL at TJ, SP Public Bridleway Blegberry. Continue along track and TL, SP Public Bridleway Blegberry. Climb this narrow track.

9 TR at TJ, no SP. **12.5km (8 miles)**

10 TL, no SP. Pass SP Unsuitable for Motors on left, for a steep descent and then climb.

11 TR at TJ (effectively SO), no SP. Pass farm on left and continue around left hand bend, for a quick descent. Take great care – there are three water culverts cut into the road, do not hit these at speed. Cross bridge and climb into Stoke.

12 TL at TJ, no SP 15km (9.5 miles). Pass Butlers Cottage on right and, further on, entrance to Hartland Abbey. Enter Hartland.

13 TR, SP Town Centre (this is the through road). Pass Shamrock café on right. Continue on B3248. **18.5km (11.5 miles)**

14 To visit the Milky Way, TR at Clares Cross. Take next TL, SO at roundabout and continue to the adventure park. Otherwise, to continue route, TL at Clares Cross, no SP.

15 TL at TJ, SP Clovelly. Descend. Follow road round to right and TR into car park to complete the route. **26km (16 miles)**

Food and drink

There is a tearoom at the Clovelly Centre, Hartland Abbey and the Milky Way.

Kings Arms, Hartland
Bar meals available.

Shamrock Café, Hartland
Typical café fare.

EXMOUTH AND BUDLEIGH SALTERTON

Route information

 Distance 26.5km (16.5 miles)

Grade Moderate

Terrain Mostly lanes, with a section of major road into Budleigh Salterton. A few climbs towards the end of the ride.

Time to allow 3–4 hours.

Getting there by car Exmouth is 11km/7 miles from Exeter, via the A376 from junction 30 of the M5.

Getting there by train Exmouth Station is on a branch line from Exeter. Telephone (0345) 484950 for information.

Starting at Exmouth Station, the route runs along the seafront before heading towards Budleigh Salterton. An unavoidable section of A road leads into the town, followed by a short section along the seafront. Then, north along a delightful valley road, partially closed to traffic, into the village of Otterton. The ride back to Exmouth has a few climbs as it passes through woods and along quiet lanes. A traffic-free track, using the disused railway track between Exmouth and Budleigh Salterton is due to open in 1999. This will be accessed approximately 200m after direction 2. For further information, contact the Tourist Information Centre in Exmouth on (01395) 263744.

Places of interest along the route

A Exmouth

Exmouth, originally a small fishing community, is one of the oldest seaside resorts in the country – it has been popular with visitors since the 18th century. The 3km (2 mile) long sea wall was constructed between 1840 and 1915 and provides a marvellous seaside promenade. For further information, telephone Exmouth Tourist information on (01395) 263744.

B Country Life, Exmouth

Large country park, featuring falconry centre, deer park and much more. Gift shop, restaurant and picnic areas. Open April to October, daily 1000–1700; July and August open until 1800. Charge. Telephone (01395) 274533.

C Fairlynch Museum, Budleigh Salterton

The Fairlynch Museum illustrates local history and supports an arts centre. Open Easter to October, daily 1400–1630. Charge. For further information, telephone the Tourist Information Centre in Budleigh Salterton on (01395) 445275.

D Otterton Mill Centre, near Budleigh Salterton

The last working water mill on the River Otter. A museum explains the working of the mill. Also craft workshops, exhibition of lace, bookshop, gallery and restaurant/bakery. Open April to October, daily 1030–1730; November to March, daily 1000–1600. Charge for admission to museum, gallery and lace exhibition. Telephone (01395) 568521.

Seafront gardens, Exmouth

Food and drink

Plenty of choice in Exmouth and Budleigh Salterton. Refreshments are also available at Country Life and Otterton Mill Centre.

Ye Olde Tythe Cottage Tearooms, Littleham
Teas, coffees and snacks.

Clinton Arms, Littleham
Bar meals available.

King's Arms, Otterton
Open all day, seven days a week. Bar and restaurant meals.

Budleigh Salterton

Route description

TR out of Exmouth Station. After 50m, TR at the roundabout, SP Docks/Seafront. Pass Exmouth Sports Centre on right. TL at next roundabout, SP Seafront. TR at TJ, SP Seafront and then TL along Esplanade. Cycle along seafront (with the sea on right).

1 SO at XR (mini roundabout), along Maer Road, no SP. Pass red postbox on right and continue along this quiet lane towards Littleham.

2 To visit Country Life, TR at TJ for a short distance. Otherwise, TL at TJ into West Down Lane, no SP.

3 TR by the church into Castle Lane, no SP (4.5km/3 miles). Continue on this road for a gradual uphill climb and cross over disused railway.

4 TR at TJ onto B3178, no SP.

5 TR at roundabout, SP Budleigh Salterton. Descend. Continue through town and SO at traffic lights. Pass church on left, Tourist Information Centre on right and then Fairlynch Museum on left. Cycle along the seafront and climb.

6 TR by war memorial and descend towards car park. **10km (6 miles)**

7 TL at TJ opposite Lime Kiln Car Park, no SP.

8 TR into South Farm Road (just before East Budleigh Road). Descend and bear right. Cross bridge.

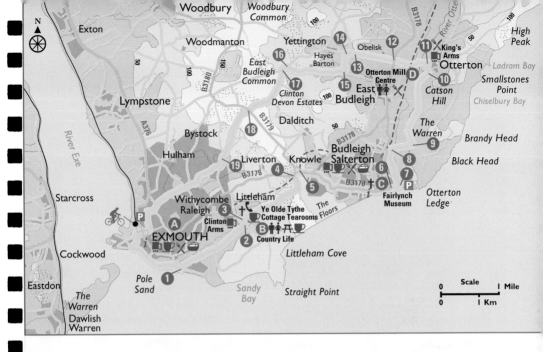

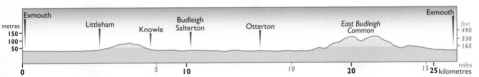

9 TL, no SP. Pass SP Road Ahead Closed – the road is closed to cars, due to irreparable subsidence, but it is quite safe for bicycles. Take care, however, as it is used as a pedestrian access for walks. Continue to Otterton.

10 TL at TJ, no SP. Descend into Otterton.

11 TL at TJ opposite seat and chestnut tree, no SP (14.5km/9 miles). Pass Otterton Mill Centre on left.

12 SO at XR (Brick Cross), no SP. Pass large obelisk on right.

13 TR at Sandy Cross (effectively SO), SP Yettington/Woodbury. Pass Bicton Arena on right.

14 TL, no SP. Pass Washmoor Barn on right. Climb.

15 TR at TJ, no SP. Pass Hayes Barton on right (birthplace of Sir Walter Raleigh, no public access).

16 TL at TJ, SP Exmouth. **19km (12 miles)**

17 TL, no SP. Cycle through Clinton Devon Estates, past tree plantations.

18 SO at XR into St John's Road, no SP. Enter Exmouth.

19 TL at TJ into Dinan Way (22.5km/14 miles). Shortly afterwards, TR and then TL into St John's Road. Continue and SO at roundabout into Withycombe Road. TR at roundabout by Phear Park, then TL at XR and continue along Exmouth's main street. Bear right past the pedestrianised area to TR, SP Exmouth/Bus/ Rail Station and complete the route. **26.5km (16.5 miles)**

STICKLEPATH, CHAGFORD AND CASTLE DROGO

Route information

 Distance 29km (18 miles)

 Grade Strenuous

 Terrain Quiet lanes throughout, with a number of short, steep climbs, particularly on the approach to Chagford.

 Time to allow 2–4 hours.

 Getting there by car Sticklepath is signed from the Okehampton bypass (A30). There is car parking in the village.

 Getting there by train There is no practical railway access to this ride.

From Sticklepath, the route skirts the scenic eastern edge of Dartmoor to the village of Gidleigh. A series of short, sharp ascents and descents takes you to the highly scenic village of Chagford. From here, a brief section of A road and a climb lead past Castle Drogo, before a series of pretty lanes take you back to Sticklepath.

Places of interest along the route

Ⓐ Finch Foundry, Sticklepath

Sticklepath (steep path) was a place of strategic importance for centuries, providing a safe crossing of the River Taw on the main route into Cornwall. At one time there were at least seven water wheels in the village, providing the power to process wool, grain and iron. Three of the four remaining wheels can be seen working at the Finch Foundry. The foundry itself dates from the 19th century and produced sickles, scythes and shovels for agriculture and mining. Tearoom. National Trust property. Open April to October, Wednesday–Monday 1100–1730. Charge. Telephone (01837) 840046.

Ⓑ Chagford

A picturesque village, with a mixture of 16th- to 19th-century houses around a village square. Chagford was a wealthy Medieval parish, through tin mining and wool, and was given the status of a stannary town, able to run its own affairs under a local judiciary.

Ⓒ Castle Drogo, near Easton

An extraordinary granite mansion, designed by Sir Edwin Lutyens and built between 1910 and 1930. The castle stands overlooking a gorge and the River Teign, with panoramic views over Dartmoor. There are landscaped gardens and woodland walks along the river. Shop, tearoom and restaurant. National Trust property. Open April to October, Saturday–Thursday 1100–1730. Charge. Telephone (01647) 433306.

Village on the edge of Dartmoor

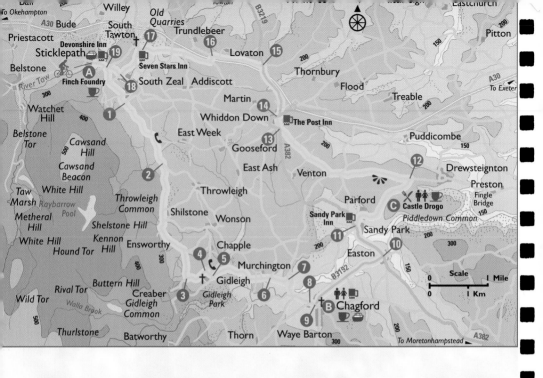

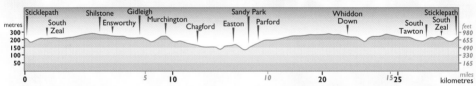

Route description

Starting opposite Sticklepath Stores, head away from Finch Foundry and out of the village.

1 TR, SP Throwleigh/Gidleigh, for a gradual uphill climb. Cross bridge and cattle grid.

2 TR, SP Shilstone/Gidleigh. Continue on this road with moorland views, following SP Gidleigh.

3 TL at Old Rectory Cross, SP Gidleigh (7km/4.5 miles). Descend a narrow, high-hedged lane.

4 TR, SP Gidleigh. Pass Gidleigh Castle (private) and church on right.

5 TL at TJ (Gidleigh Cross), SP Murchington/Chagford.

6 TR at Chagford Cross, SP Chagford.

7 TR at TJ, SP Chagford (11km/7 miles). At XR follow road to left (no turn as such). Enter Chagford.

8 TL at TJ (effectively SO), SP Parish Church.

9 TL, SP Moretonhampstead/Okehampton. Leave Chagford, passing fire station on right.

10 TL at XR, SP Moretonhampstead.

Castle Drogo

11 TR at XR, SP Drewsteignton/Fingle Bridge (15km/9.5 miles). Climb and pass entrance to Castle Drogo on right.

12 TL at TJ, SP Whiddon Down/ Okehampton, for a gentle climb. Road flattens out with occasional views to left. Continue on this road towards Whiddon Down.

13 TR at TJ (Toll Hose Cross), SP Okehampton/Exeter (22km/13.5 miles). Then TR along Turnpike Road, over speed bumps.

14 SO at XR, SP Spreyton/North Tawton. Cross dual carriageway (Okehampton bypass).

15 TL at Brandis Cross, no SP.

16 TL at Ringhill Cross, no SP. Recross bypass. TR at TJ, SP South Tawton. Pass stone cross on right. Arrive South Tawton.

27km (17 miles)

17 TR, no SP, then TL at TJ, opposite church.

18 TR at TJ, SP Sticklepath.

19 TR at TJ, SP Okehampton. Continue into Sticklepath to complete the route.

29km (18 miles)

Food and drink

Tearoom, pub and shops in Chagford. Refreshments are also available at Finch Foundry and Castle Drogo. There are pubs in South Tawton, Whiddon Down and a convenience store at Sticklepath.

 Devonshire Inn, Sticklepath
Bar meals available.

 The Post Inn, Widdon Down
Pub food available.

LYNTON, LYNMOUTH AND THE VALLEY OF THE ROCKS

Route information

Distance 33.5km (21 miles)

Grade Strenuous

Terrain The first half of the route is on a narrow, heavily undulating road with several steep climbs. The return to Lynton is along a quiet and altogether flatter A road.

Time to allow 3–4 hours.

Getting there by car Lynton is off the A39 Barnstable to Minehead road. There is a pay and display car park 100m from the Tourist Information Centre. TR out of the car park to start the route.

Getting there by train There is no practical railway access to this ride.

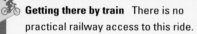

From the town of Lynton, the route heads west through the scenically splendid Valley of the Rocks. This part of the route follows the usual rule of cycling – for good views a degree of climbing and descending is necessary. The Valley of Rocks and the sea views at Lee Bay and Woody Bay are spectacular. The road through the valley is on a narrow toll road (no charge for bicycles), so it is not much used by cars. The Hunters Inn at Martinhoe provides a convenient stop, after which the route climbs to meet the A road back into Lynton. You may take this route, or simply return back along the toll road for a different angle on the wonderful scenery.

Route description

Start with the Tourist Information Centre behind you. Cycle right, pass row of guest houses on right and post office on left. Leave Lynton and follow SP the Valley of Rocks. Pass cricket ground on right. Continue on this road and cycle past the stunning rock formations on the right. SO at small roundabout and onto the narrow toll road. Pass Lee Abbey (Christian conference centre) on right. Road drops steeply. Pass tearooms at foot of hill. Continue and pass hotel.

1 TR at TJ (effectively SO), no SP.

6.5km (4 miles)

2 TR at XR, SP Hunters Inn/Heddons Mouth/ Trentishoe, for a steep descent.

3 Arrive TJ with Hunters Inn on right of junction. TR at TJ, SP Coombe Martin/ Barnstaple (9.5km/6 miles). Continue on this road.

4 TL at TJ, SP Blackmoor Gate A399/ Lynton/ South Molton/Simonsbath.

16.5km (10.5 miles)

5 TL onto A39, SP Lynmouth/Lynton (21km/13 miles). Continue on this road towards Lynton.

6 TL, SP Lynton B3234/Youth Hostel.

31.5km (19.5 miles)

7 TL, SP Lynton, and climb. Wonderful views over Lynmouth to the right. Follow road as it bends left, SP Town Centre/Valley of Rocks/ Car Park. Continue along Crossmead (one way street.) TR at TJ, SP Town Centre/Hospital/ Health Centre/ Tourist Information Centre and complete the route. **33.5km (21 miles)**

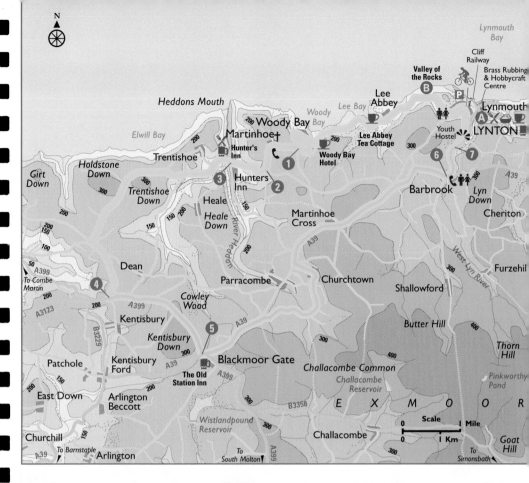

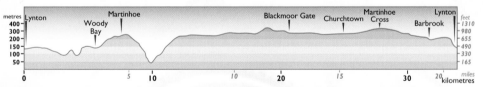

Food and drink

There are lots of places to choose from in Lynton and Lynmouth, and a pub in Blackmoor Gate.

Lee Abbey Tea Cottage, Lee Abbey
Egon Ronay recommended, in a great setting.

Woody Bay Hotel, Woody Bay
Morning coffee and afternoon tea served.

Hunters Inn, Martinhoe
A popular pub in an idyllic setting. Good food and outdoor seating.

Valley of the Rocks

Places of interest along the route

A Lynton and Lynmouth

This area has been described as England's Switzerland. Lynton is a picturesque harbourside village and Lynton, 274m (900 feet) above, offers marvellous coastal views. The **Cliff Railway**, the only working water-powered Victorian railway in Europe, links the two villages. Stunning views as the track rises 153m (500 feet) through a gradient of 1:1¾. Refreshments available. Open all year, Monday–Saturday 0800–1900, Sunday 1000–1900. Charge. Telephone (01598) 753486. Just to the east of Lynton is **Watersmeet**, a beautiful wooded gorge with a restored 19th-century Gothic fishing lodge. Tearoom and shop. National Trust property. Open April to September, daily 1030–1730; October, daily 1030–1630. Admission free. Telephone (01598) 753348. The **Brass Rubbing and Hobbycraft Centre** in Lynmouth has a selection of over 100 facsimiles of monumental brasses and visitors can make their own rubbing. Also craft shop. Open Easter to September, Monday–Friday 1100–1630; open daily during school holidays. Admission free with charge for rubbings. Telephone (01598) 752529.

B Valley of the Rocks

Spectacular rock formations situated above the cliffs of north Devon.

Route information

Distance 35km (21.5 miles)

Grade Moderate

Terrain Mostly flat, quiet roads and lanes. One steep descent and climb out of St Mawgan.

Time to allow 2–4 hours.

Getting there by car Roche is signed from the A39, midway between Bodmin and Indian Queens. There is car parking at the station and in the town.

Getting there by train Roche Station is on the Bodmin to Newquay line. Telephone (0345) 484950 for further information.

From Roche Station, the route heads north west along minor roads, passing the hill fort of Castle an Dinas and on to St Columb Major and St Mawgan. The return is along quiet lanes, far removed from the hustle and bustle of the A roads that cross this area.

Places of interest along the route

Ⓐ Roche

Roche is an old clay mining village. Just outside the village, 0.5km (0.3 mile) to the east, is Roche Rock, a 14th-century hermitage perched on a granite outcrop, associated with the leper St Gonand.

Ⓑ Castle an Dinas

Covering an area of 7 hectares (17 acres) and standing at 213m (700 feet) high, this Iron Age fort is one of the largest in Cornwall and commands extensive views. The castle was occupied from 400BC through to 150AD. Cornish legend says that this was the seat of the Dark Ages Dukes of Cornwall, between the 5th and 10th centuries. Well worth the climb. There are two tracks approaching the castle, close and parallel to each other – use the one on the left.

Ⓒ St Columb Major

Attractive town, home to a Medieval game – hurling the silver ball. Two teams of several hundred people each (the townsmen against the countrymen) attempt to carry a silver ball made of applewood through goals set 3km (2 miles) apart. The game is played on Shrove Tuesday and on the Saturday, eleven days later, with such enthusiasm that shopfronts are boarded up.

Ⓓ St Mawgan

St Mawgan lies in the Vale of Lanherne. The pub, the Falcon, is said to have been named during the Reformation, when it was common for a bird to be released into the air as a sign that a secret Catholic mass was to take place. The village church contains one of the finest collection of brasses in the country. The village is also home to the **Japanese Garden and Bonsai Nursery**. Described as an 'oasis of tranquillity', this is an authentic Japanese garden with water and Zen gardens, and traditional Japanese plants. Also nursery stocking a huge selection of Bonsai. Open all year, daily 1000–1800. Charge for admission to garden. Telephone (01637) 860116.

St Columb

Food and drink

There are several places for refreshment in Roche and St Columb.

Falcon Inn, St Mawgan
Village pub serving bar meals.

Post Office, St Mawgan
Combined post office, village store and tearoom.

Route description

TL out of station and cycle into Roche.

1 TL at roundabout, then TR, SP Redruth (avoiding low bridge).

2 TR, SP Redruth/Tregoss.

3 TR at TJ, SP Newquay.

4 TR at TJ, SP Bodmin, then immediately TL. Pass Castle an Dinas on right (6.5km/4 miles). Continue west on this road.

5 Take third exit at roundabout, SP St Columb. *9.5km (6 miles)*

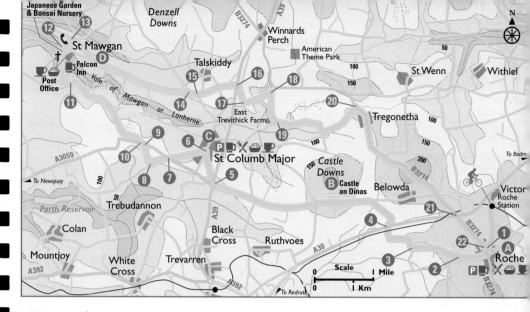

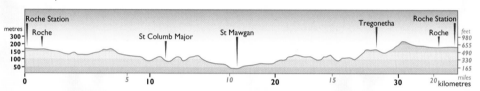

6	TL, SP Newquay.

7	SO at XR, SP Tregaswith.

8	TR into a narrow lane, no SP.

9	TL at TJ, no SP.

10 TR, SP St Mawgan. Continue towards St Mawgan.

11 TR, SP St Mawgan (16km/10 miles). Descend into village. Cross bridge and pass Japanese Garden and Bonsai Nursery on left.

12 TR (hard right turn), no SP, and climb. Follow road as it swings left and climbs again.

13 TR at XR, SP St Columb/Wadebridge, and continue.

14	TR at TJ (effectively SO), SP St Columb.

15 TL, SP Talskiddy. *21.5km (13.5 miles)*

16	SO at XR, across A39.

17	TL, SP Tregamere/Tregonetha.

18 TR on left hand bend, no SP (24.5km/ 15 miles). Continue along a grass-centred lane.

19	TL at TJ, no SP. Pass East Trevithick Farm.

20 TR at TJ onto B3274, no SP (28km/ 17.5 miles). Continue towards Roche.

21	SO at XR, SP Redruth/St Austell.

22 TL at roundabout and return to the station and the end of the route. *35km (21.5 miles)*

KINGSBRIDGE, SALCOMBE AND SLAPTON SANDS

Route information

Distance 39km (24 miles)

Grade Strenuous

Terrain Undulating narrow lanes, some steep. Two off-road sections, the second of which is testing and muddy.

Time to allow 4–7 hours.

Getting there by car Kingsbridge is off the A381, Totnes to Plymouth road. There are several pay and display car parks – choose the one next to the Tourist Information Centre.

Getting there by train There is no practical railway access to this ride.

This route starts in Kingsbridge and heads south to Salcombe, along a hilly but quiet backroad. Take the passenger ferry across Salcombe Harbour and, after an initial climb, a flat road takes you into East Prawle. A bridlepath ending in a glorious descent into a wooded valley follows, before a further descent into Torcross. The route continues with a windswept ride along Slapton Sands, before returning to Kingsbridge via a challenging off-road section along an unclassified road.

Places of interest along the route

Ⓐ Kingsbridge

Situated at the head of Kingsbridge Estuary, Kingsbridge was a prosperous Medieval market town. The Shambles (once the meat market), with imposing stone pillars, dates back to 1585.

Also 18th-century coaching inn, the Kings Arms. A craft market is held at the town hall, Easter to Christmas, Tuesday and Friday. For further information, telephone Kingsbridge Tourist Information Centre on (01548) 853195.

Ⓑ Salcombe

Beautifully situated one-time fishing village and now a mecca for sailors. The village lies inland and its sheltered position gives it one of the mildest climates in the country. The **Maritime Museum** illustrates the seafaring history of Salcombe and the surrounding area. Open April to October, daily 1030–1230 and 1430–1630. Charge. Telephone Salcombe Tourist Information Centre for further information on (01548) 843927. The ferry from Salcombe runs all year, daily between 0800 and 1800. Telephone the Tourist Information Centre to confirm times.

Ⓒ Slapton Sands

A natural causeway separating the seawater of Start Bay and the freshwater lagoon of Slapton Ley. Slapton Ley is a nature reserve and bird-watchers paradise, home to native and migrating birds, freshwater fish, insects and plants. During the Second World War the area around Slapton was used as a training area for the D-Day landings. In April 1944 a German E boat attacked the beach, killing over 600 American servicemen. A Sherman tank stands in memorial to this tragedy. For further information, telephone Salcombe Tourist Information Centre, number above.

Ⓓ Stancombe Cider Farm, near Sherford

Situated on an idyllic estate, now orchards and holiday accommodation. Over 600 apple trees provide fruit for the production of cider by traditional methods, using a 200-year-old cider press. Also tearoom serving cream teas. Open all year, daily 1000–1700. Admission free. Telephone (01548) 531634.

Salcombe, from East Portlemouth

Food and drink

There are lots of places to choose from in Kingsbridge and Salcombe, and shops in Kellaton, Torcross and Slapton. Refreshments also available at Stancombe Cider Farm.

Godolphin Cottage, Portlemouth

Small shop selling drinks and basic groceries.

The Free Booter, East Prawle

The pub has two open fires, one allegedly surrounded by a captain's cabin door from a local wreck. Garden with sea views. Children welcome. Basic menu.

Pigs Nose Inn, East Prawle

Bar meals available.

Village Inn, Torcross

Spacious inn with open fire. Food served at lunch times. Also accommodation.

Start Bay Inn, Torcross

Serves food all day. There is almost a café-like atmosphere in the family room.

Queen's Arms, Slapton

Small, beamed small pub with open fire. Food available.

Tower Inn, Slapton

Pub adjacent to a tower, the remains of a 13th-century church. Open fires. Food available.

Route description

Start at the Tourist Information Centre in Kingsbridge and follow SP Plymouth/Salcombe/Totnes uphill. TL just past Shell Garage, into Rope Walk. Pass cattle market on left and descend, leaving Kingsbridge. Cycle along the hilly, undulating lane with intermittent views of the estuary to the left.

1 TL at TJ, SP Batson/Salcombe.

2 TL at XR, SP Lincombe/Lower Batson, for a flat section along a ridge. **5km (3 miles)**

3 TR, SP Batson/Salcombe. Steep descent into Salcombe – at the bottom of the hill there is a good view along the estuary.

4 TL, no SP. Continue along right side of the estuary on flat road.

5 TL along Island Street. Pass chandleries on left and follow road as it swings 90 degrees to right, towards the church.

6 TL at TJ, no SP. Head downhill, past the Tourist Information Centre and museum on the right.

7 TL, SP (on the wall of Midland/HSBC Bank) Ferry Inn/Ferry Boats. Descend the steps and wait for the ferry.

8 On the other side, TL, no SP.

9 TR, no SP – this is a hard TR with Clay Park house on left (9km/5.5 miles). Climb. Pass Godolphin Cottage on right. Opposite are great views of the estuaries. Pass church, after which the road flattens out.

10 TR, SP East Prawle.

11 TR at TJ, SP East Prawle (SP obscured by house on right). **13.5km (8.5 miles)**

12 TL, no SP (public toilets and telephone on right). Pass between Grunters Café and the Pigs Nose Inn. Descend, bear left to TR, no SP, and pass the Saddle (house) on left. Cycle through East Prawle.

13 TR just before telephone box on right. The tarmac road becomes a bridleway.
14.5km (9 miles)

14 TR, SP Public Bridleway/Lannacombe Green/Woodcombe Sand. Follow the diverted bridleway around farm, following SP Lannacombe Green. Cross field and head for gate just to left of pond.

15 TR at TJ, SP Public Bridleway. SO at XR of bridleways (18km/11 miles). Pass farm on right and follow SP Lannacombe Green, ignoring track going downhill to left. Follow blue arrows into a steep drop to the bottom of the valley.

16 TR at TJ onto tarmac, no SP.

17 TL at TJ, SP Kellaton/Stokenham, and enter Kellaton.

18 TL at TJ, SP Stokenham/Torcross/Kingsbridge.

19 SO at XR (more of a five-way cross), SP Stokenham/Torcross/Kingsbridge (20.5km/12.5 miles). Continue on this road.

20 TR at XR, no SP, passing Mattiscombe Farm and later Torcross Viewpoint on left – good view along Slapton Sands from here. Descend steep hill.

21 TR at TJ, no SP, along Slapton Sands (24.5km/15 miles). Pass tank memorial on left.

22 TL, SP Slapton, and enter Slapton. Follow road as it bends to right, SP Totnes.

23 TL at Brookstreet Cross, no SP.

24 RHF, no SP, and pass Church View House on right. Climb.

25 SO at XR, SP Stokenham/Chillington.

26 TR, SP Start, and continue.

27 SO at XR, no SP but red post box in wall to right of junction (29.5km/18.5 miles). Climb. The road becomes a bridlepath by a farm entrance, where continue SO (muddy). Cross stream (31.5km/19.5 miles) for a hard climb out. Reach a better surface and rejoin tarmac where:

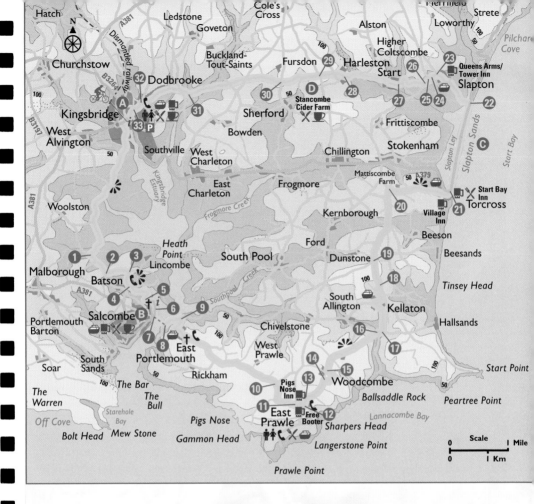

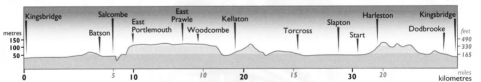

28 TR at TJ (effectively SO), no SP (Brockford House on right). Then after 100m, TL (effectively SO) and climb.

29 SO at XR, SP Stancombe/Kingsbridge. Pass Stancombe Cider Farm.

30 SO at XR (Stancombe Cross), no SP (33.5km/21 miles). Continue on this road.

31 TR, no SP, and climb (36.5km/22.5 miles). Pass Coombes Cross and enter Kingsbridge.

32 TL at XR, no SP but telephone on left of junction.

33 TL at TJ, no SP. Continue through Kingsbridge and finish the route at the Tourist Information Centre.   ***39km (24 miles)***

THE LIZARD PENINSULA

Route information

Distance 40km (25 miles)

Grade Moderate

Terrain A series of quiet lanes with two climbs. The rest of the ride is fairly flat, with a section of A and B road.

Time to allow 3–4 hours.

Getting there by car Coverack is on the south east of the Lizard Peninsular. From Helston, take the A3083 SP the Lizard, then take the B3293 after RNAS Culdrose. There is car parking throughout the village – the best car park to use is that at the north end of the village (the opposite end to the harbour).

Getting there by train There is no practical railway access to this ride.

This route covers the central and eastern area of the Lizard Peninsula, designated an Area of Outstanding Natural Beauty. Coverack is a picturesque, traditional fishing village. The route climbs out of Coverack to the village of St Keverne, and then drops back to the coast at Porthallow. A steady climb leads to a trig point and a panoramic view of the Lizard Peninsula. From here, the road flattens out as you head west towards the huge satellite dishes at Goonhilly. If time allows, it is worth the detour all the way to Lizard Point. The route heads east across Goonhilly Downs, before returning to Coverack.

Places of interest along the route

Ⓐ Roskilly's, St Keverne

A working farm featuring conservation area with ponds, woods and meadow. Visitors can see the Jersey herd being milked (daily, 1615–1715). Tearooms serving snacks and farm-made icecream. Also shop selling gifts produced on the farm. Open May to September, daily 1000–2030; October to April, telephone to confirm opening. Admission free. Telephone (01326) 280479.

Ⓑ Porthallow Vineyard, Porthallow

Vineyard and herb garden. Self-guided tour and free tastings of wines, ciders and liqueurs. Shop. Open Easter to September, Monday–Saturday 1100–1300 and 1400–1800; October, Monday–Saturday 1100–1300 and 1400–1700; November, Monday–Saturday 1400–1700; December, Friday and Saturday 1400–1700. Telephone (01326) 260050.

Ⓒ Trelowarren

The Trelowarren Estate has been owned by the same family since 1427. Occupied by the army during the Second World War, the house and grounds are now undergoing restoration. There is plenty to see and do. The Lizard Countryside Centre introduces visitors to the Lizard Peninsula, its people, landscape, flora and fauna, through photography, touch screen computers and computer imaging. Open Easter to September, daily 1100–1700. Admission free. Telephone (01326) 221661. Waymarked woodland walks cross the estate, visiting the quay and Halliggye Fogou. Picnics welcome. The gardens at Trelowarren were developed during the 18th century and are being rebuilt and restored to the original design. Walks and gardens open Easter to September, daily 1100–1700. Admission free. Tours of the house are offered Easter to September, Wednesdays and Bank Holiday Mondays, 1415–1700. Charge. Telephone (01326) 221366. The Cornwall Crafts Association has a gallery with a permanent display of Cornish crafts and an annual programme of changing exhibitions. Pottery and weaving studio. Open Easter to September, telephone (01326) 221567 to confirm times. Also Yard Restaurant serving coffee, lunches and evening meals.

Ⓓ Lizard National Nature Reserve, Goonhilly Downs

Nature reserve of international botanic importance – fifteen of Britain's rarest plants grow here. The soil of serpentine rock and a mild maritime climate support a wide variety of habitats, home to many wild creatures. This is the hunting ground of Hen Harriers and Short Eared Owls. Cornish heath flowers in the late summer – the controlled burning and grazing by Exmoor ponies allow smaller plants to flower.

Ⓔ Earth Station Goonhilly, Goonhilly Downs

The largest satellite station on earth. Visitor centre, multi media command centre and internet zone. Also restaurant and children's play area. Open April to November, daily 1000–1700. Charge. Telephone 0800 679593.

Lizard Point

Route description

Start at the harbour in Coverack. Cycle along the seafront, passing shops on left, and climb out of village, passing long stay car park on left.

1 TR at XR, SP Trevalsoe. Pass Roskilly's.
4km (2.5 miles)

2 TL at XR, SP St Keverne, and continue into St Keverne.

3 TL at TJ opposite St Keverne newsagents, no SP. Then TR in the central square, SP Manaccan/Helford/Porthallow (4.5km/3 miles). Leave St Keverne, following SP Porthallow. Pass Porthallow Vineyard on right and continue into Porthallow. Pass entrance to beach and SO out of village, ignoring turn to the right. Climb through a narrow wooded lane.

4 TR at TJ and keep climbing.
9.5km (6 miles)

5 TL at TJ, SP Porthoustock/St Keverne. The trig point opposite this junction is worth climbing for panoramic views.

6 TR at TJ (effectively SO), SP Newtown/Helston. Go through Tregidden and enter Newtown in St Martin.

7 TL, SP Helston.
15.5km (9.5 miles)

8 TR at TJ, SP Helston.

9 To visit Trelowarren TR. Otherwise, TL opposite entrance to Trelowarren, no SP (18.5km/11.5 miles). Continue to Cross Lanes.

10 TL at XR onto A3083, SP Lizard.

11 To visit Lizard Point, continue SO for around trip of 14km (8.5 miles). Otherwise, TL just after Mullion Park, no SP (25.5km/16 miles). Pass football posts on left and continue.

12 TL at TJ, SP Helston/St Keverne/Goonhilly/Coverack, and cycle across Goonhilly Downs.

13 TL to visit Lizard National Nature Reserve and Earth Station Goonhilly. Otherwise, TR at XR, SP St Keverne.
33.5km (21 miles)

14 TR, SP Penhallick/Treleaver.

15 TL, SP Coverack, for a steep descent back into Coverack and the end of the ride.
40km (25 miles)

Food and drink

There are shops, tearooms and a pub in Coverack. Also plenty of choice in St Keverne and Porthallow, and pubs in Newtown in St Martin and Cross Lanes. Refreshments are also available at Roskilly's, Trelowarren and Earth Station Goonhilly.

The Croust House, Roskilly's
Cream teas and home-made meals.

Taranaki Tea Gardens, Porthallow
Delightful tearoom located in a garden.

Mullion Park Holiday Park, near Penhale
Supermarket, pub and shop selling afternoon tea.

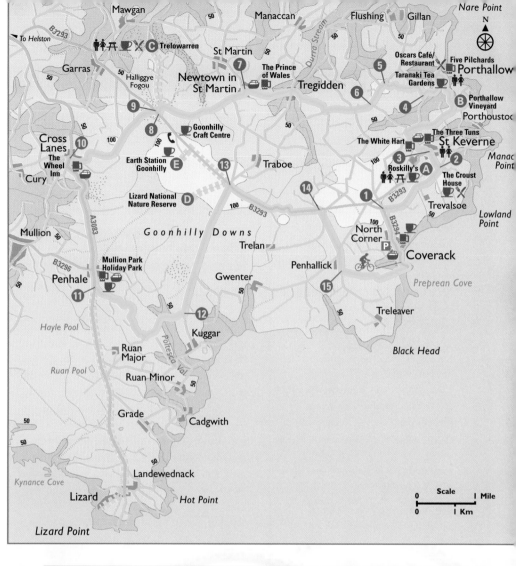

Mawgan
Manaccan
Flushing
Gillan
Nare Point
N
To Helston
B3293
50
Trelowarren
50
50
Garras
50
Halliggye
Fogou
50
St Martin
The Prince
of Wales
Tregidden
Oscars Café/
Restaurant
Taranaki Tea
Gardens
Five Pilchards
Porthallow
Newtown in
St Martin
Porthallow
Vineyard
Porthoustoc
Goonhilly
Craft Centre
50
The White Hart
The Three Tuns
St Keverne
Manac
Point
Cross
Lanes
100
Earth Station
Goonhilly
Traboe
100
Roskilly's
The Croust
House
The
Wheel
Inn
Cury
Lizard National
Nature Reserve
100
B3293
Trevalsoe
Lowland
Point
Mullion
50
A3083
Goonhilly Downs
Trelan
100
North
Corner
Coverack
Penhallick
Preprean Cove
B3296
Mullion Park
Holiday Park
Gwenter
Penhale
50
50
Kuggar
Treleaver
Hayle Pool
50
Black Head
Ruan
Major
Poltesca Val.
Ruan Pool
Ruan Minor
50
Grade
Cadgwith
50
50
Landewednack
50
Kynance Cove
Lizard
Hot Point
Lizard Point

Scale
0   1 Mile
0   1 Km

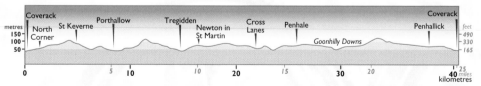

Coverack
North
Corner
St Keverne
Porthallow
Tregidden
Newton in
St Martin
Cross
Lanes
Penhale
Coverack
Penhallick
metres
150
100
50
Goonhilly Downs
feet
490
330
165
0   5   10   10   20   15   30   20   40 25
miles
kilometres

TAVISTOCK AND BURRATOR RESERVOIR

Route information

Distance 45km (28 miles)

Grade Strenuous

Terrain Undulating sections of open moorland with extensive views – an optional off-road section is included across the southern moor. The hard climbs throughout the route are punctuated by flatter sections, with one fast descent.

Time to allow 3–6 hours.

Getting there by car Tavistock is the major town on the western edge of Dartmoor, on the A386. A long stay car park (charge) is signed from the town centre as Meadowlands Leisure. To reach the start of the route at Bedford Square, TR out of the car park for 300m.

Getting there by train There is no practical railway access to this ride.

Starting from the Tourist Information Centre in Tavistock, the route heads out over Whitchurch Down and through the beautiful lanes that line the western edge of Dartmoor. You continue on through Sampford Spiney and Walkhampton before descending for a circuit of Burrator Reservoir. An off-road section follows, across the moor to Princetown. The last part of the
ride traverses the road that divides the moor in two, with the wilder, more remote north moor to the right and the softer southern moor to the left. A fast descent takes you back to Tavistock

Places of interest along the route

A Tavistock

The town originally grew up around a Benedictine Abbey, founded in 974AD. After the Dissolution, the Russell family, later the Dukes of Bedford, were given much of the abbey land, and the town's wealth grew on wood mills, foundries and tanneries. Today Tavistock is a pleasant market town, supporting the large farming community of the surrounding area. The town was granted a market charter in 1105 and regular markets are still held today. **Tavistock Museum** illustrates local history through permanent and changing exhibitions. Open Easter to October, Wednesday 1400–1600, Friday and Saturday 1000–1200 and 1400–1600. Charge. Telephone (01822) 612546. Tavistock Tourist Information Centre can be contacted on (01822) 612938.

B Burrator Reservoir, near Yelverton

A dam was constructed here in 1898, close to Devonport Leat. The leat was constructed by Sir Francis Drake with labour from troops captured during the Napoleonic Wars, its purpose to improve the water supply to Devonport in Plymouth. The reservoir is surrounded by open moorland and mixed woodland, and a network of footpaths and bridleways. Ice cream and snack vans during the summer. Telephone (01837) 871335.

Ⓒ Princetown

The village sits at over 427m (1400 feet) above sea level in an exposed area of Dartmoor. Famous for its prison, completed in 1809 by prisoners of the Napoleonic Wars. The prison held hundreds of French and American inmates, and closed in 1816 after the cessation of hostilities. It was reopened in 1850 and continues in use today. There is a Dartmoor National Park Centre in the old prison officers' club. For further information, telephone the Tourist Information Centre at Tavistock.

Food and drink

Tavistock and Princetown have numerous cafés and pubs. There is a pub and convenience store in Walkhampton.

Burrator Inn, Dousland
Serves good basic pub food.

Two Bridges Hotel, Two Bridges
Beautiful setting, comfy armchairs and excellent value cream teas served after 1500. Also outdoor seating.

Dartmoor Inn, Merrivale
Outside seating, a log fire, and food in this lovely pub on the moor.

Burrator Reservoir and Dam

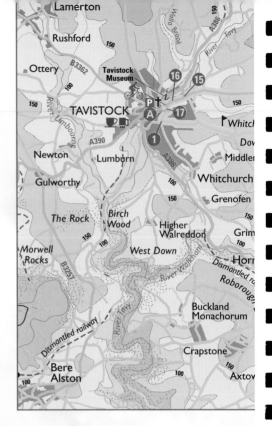

Start at the front of the Tourist Information Centre, facing the Parish Church across the road. Cycle left, SO at mini roundabout (with Post Office on right). Cross the River Tavy. TR at next mini roundabout and climb the hill.

1 TL into Down Road, SP Whitchurch Down. Climb steadily on this wide residential road. Cross cattle grid. Follow road as it swings left, passing golf club on left. Enter Dartmoor National Park, staying on road as it swings right (through 90 degrees) and goes through centre of golf course. There are usually a lot of Dartmoor Ponies in this area. SO at Warrens Cross (4km/2.5 miles). Stay on road as it continues across open moorland.

2 This turn is easy to miss – pass to left of white house and just after brown SP Dartmoor on right (before road narrows between two walls), TR, no SP (7.5km/5 miles). Pass Sampford Spiney Church on left.

3 TR at TJ, no SP.

4 TR at TJ, SP Walkhampton. Cross cattle grid.

5 TL at XR (red telephone box on right of this junction), SP Walkhampton (10.5km/6.5 miles). Steep descent, cross Huckworthy Bridge and climb into Walkhampton.

6 TL by war memorial, SP Dousland/ Princetown. Climb.

7 SO at XR into Burrator Road, SP Meavy/ Sheepstor.

8 TL, SP Sheepstor/Burrator Reservoir. Road is flat then descends to reservoir (15.5km/9.5 miles). Follow road to right, SP Sheepstor, and cross dam. Continue into Sheepstor.

9 TL, no SP. Pass Byeways (house name) on left. Cross Norseworthy Bridge. Continue alongside and then around eastern edge of reservoir.

10 TR, no SP, for a steep climb. Cross leat. To continue route, continue on road as it follows leat downstream on left. Cross leat again and stay on road as it drops below leat.

For off-road section, TR onto rough track when road swings left (keeping leat on right). Cross leat via clapper bridge and follow track over River Meavy. Bear left then RHF after 50m. TL uphill at TJ by end of plantation. Head for a gate leading to open moorland where continue uphill to recross leat. Continue SO and when arrive at tarmac, TL, no SP. Cycle into Princetown and rejoin route at direction 13 where TR at mini round-about.

11 TR at TJ, no SP. As road descends, Brentor Church appears ahead. Cross cattle grid.

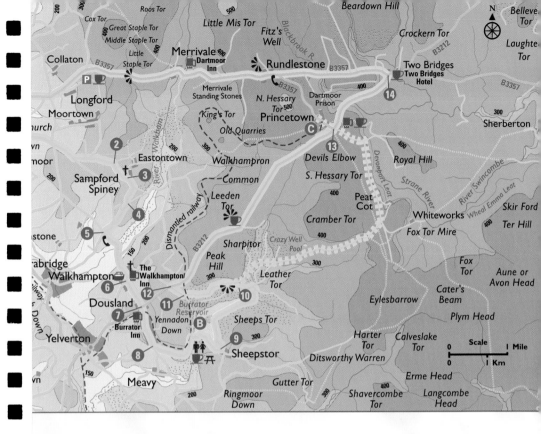

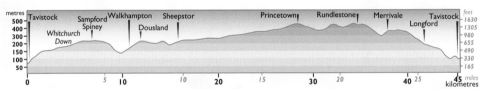

12 TR at TJ, SP Princetown B3212. Climb. Cross cattle grid and continue onto open moor. Top of hill reached (23.5km/14.5 miles). Continue on this road into Princetown.

13 To visit Princetown, SO at mini roundabout. Otherwise TR at roundabout into Two Bridges Road, SP Moretonhampstead/Two Bridges/Dartmeet. Cross cattle grid. **30.5km (19 miles)**

14 TL at TJ, SP Tavistock B3357. Cross two cattle grids. Pass Merrivale Standing Stones on left (35.5km/22 miles). Descend into Merrivale

(comprising quarry and pub). Continue on this road, with a fast descent down Pork Hill. Pass SP Leaving Dartmoor National Park (41km/25.5 miles) and arrive Tavistock.

15 TL at TJ, SP Town Centre.

16 TL at roundabout, SP Plymouth/Town Centre.

17 TR at roundabout, SP Plymouth/Liskeard/Launceston/Town Centre and continue back to Tourist Information Centre to complete the route. **45km (28 miles)**

LYDFORD AND BRENT TOR

Route information

Distance 47km (29 miles)

Grade Moderate

Terrain Single track roads and hedged Devon lanes. One hard climb out of Chillaton.

Time to allow 3–6 hours.

Getting there by car Take the A386 from the A30. Peter Tavy is signed just north east of Tavistock. Park in the village.

Getting there by train There is no practical railway access to this ride.

This route takes an undulating single track road from Peter Tavy, as it winds its way along the western moor to Mary Tavy. On to Lydford and Lydford Gorge, for a delightful ride along part of the West Devon Cycleway to Chillaton. A steep climb follows, towards Brentor Church, followed by a gradual descent back to Peter Tavy.

Places of interest along the route

Ⓐ Lydford

Established by King Alfred to defend the surrounding countryside against Viking attacks. **Lydford Castle** was originally constructed by the Normans in the 11th century. Later a keep was built on the site and used by the Dartmoor tin miners as a court and prison. English Heritage property. Access at all reasonable times. Admission free. Telephone 0171-973 3434 for further information. **Lydford Gorge**, owned by the National Trust, is 2.5km (1.5 miles) long. There are woodland walks along the top of the gorge, leading down to the 27m (90 feet) White Lady Waterfall. Shop and tearoom. Open April to October, daily 1000–1730. Charge (reduced admission for cyclists). Telephone (01822) 820320.

Ⓑ Brentor Church

A local landmark that can be seen from miles away. Brent Tor is the remains of a volcanic plug and stands 335m (1100 feet) above sea level. A church was first built on this site in 1130 and the present building dates mostly from the 13th and 15th centuries. Legend has it that the Devil moved the church onto the hill to prevent people from attending. The panoramic views from the top make the walk worth the effort. For further information, contact Tavistock Tourist Information Centre on (01822) 612938.

Brentor Church

Route description

Start in the centre of Peter Tavy, by the church. With your back to the church, cycle left and uphill towards the edge of the moor. Pass seat on left and continue along undulating, narrow lane with the moor on the right.

1 TL, SP Hilltown/Willsworthy and descend. Cross Hill Bridge and climb.

2 TL, SP Horndon/Mary Tavy (4.5km/3 miles). Cross cattle grid onto open moorland. Continue and cross another cattle grid. Pass chapel and, a little further on, pub on left. Continue towards Mary Tavy.

3 TR at TJ, SP Tavistock/Okehampton. Enter Mary Tavy.

4 SO at XR, no SP (9.5km/6 miles). Pass to right of Methodist Church.

5 TR at XR, no SP. Pass Crossings Close (house name) on right. Cross cattle grid and enter open ground. A good view of Brentor Church opens out, just before descending to cross another cattle grid.

6 TR, no SP. Climb, following road as it swings to left (90 degrees) and descends. Cross cattle grid and old railway bridge.

7 TR at TJ, SP Lydford (14.5km/9 miles). Pass summer entrance to Lydford Gorge. Recross disused railway, pass pub and main entrance to Lydford Gorge on left. Steep short climb into Lydford and pass Lydford Castle on left.

8 TL at war memorial, SP Coryton (20km/12.5 miles). Cycle along typical Devon hedged lane (this is part of the West Devon Cycleway). Pass Lydford Wood on left. Continue on this road as it gradually descends, ignoring all turns.

9 SO at XR, SP Sydenham/Portgate.

28km (17.5 miles)

10 TL, SP Sydenham/Marystow (30km/18.5 miles). Cross small bridge. Bear left in front of Sydenham House.

11 TR at TJ, SP Chillaton. Cross bridge and climb.

12 TL at TJ, SP Chillaton/Tavistock and continue into Chillaton.

13 TL at TJ opposite Chichester Arms, no SP.

14 Immediately, TR, no SP, up steep single track road. Pass brown cycleway SP on right.

15 TL at TJ, no SP but brown cycleway SP on right. Continue, passing SP Quither on left.

16 TL at XR, SP Brentor (35.5km/22 miles). Continue on this straight road, the moor and Brentor Church in sight.

17 TR at TJ, SP Tavistock/Hurdwick. Pass entrance to Brentor Church on left.

18 TL at XR, no SP (just after TL SP South Brentor). Pass Trehill Cottage on right. Cycle gently downhill with good views of moor ahead. Pass large stone milestone on left.

41.5km (26 miles)

19 TL at TJ onto A386, SP Okehampton/Mary Tavy.

20 TR, SP Peter Tavy. Pass Harford Bridge Campsite on right. Continue into Peter Tavy and complete the route.   *47km (29 miles)*

Food and drink

There are several pubs in Peter Tavy, Mary Tavy and Chillaton. Refreshments are also available at Lydford Gorge.

Peter Tavy Inn, Peter Tavy
A lovely 16th-century beamed pub serving excellent food.

Mucky Duck, Lydford
Good basic food.

The Castle, Lydford
Bar meals available.

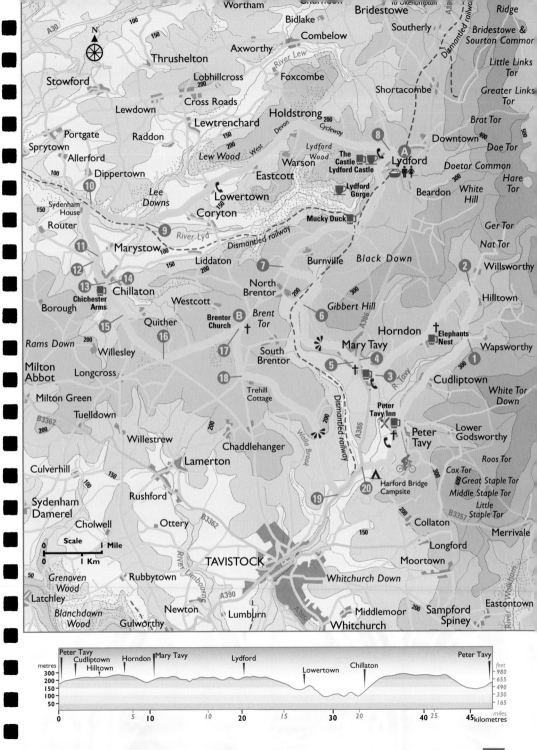

Route information

 Distance 54km (33.5 miles)

 Grade Moderate

 Terrain Mostly quiet narrow lanes, gradual in gradient. Two steep hills.

 Time to allow 3–5 hours.

 Getting there by car Tiverton is just off the A361 north Devon link road (reached from junction 27 of the M5). Follow SP Town Centre and Tourist Information. The pay and display car park by the Tourist Information Centre is the most convenient.

 Getting there by train Tiverton Parkway Station is 7.5km (5miles) from Tiverton. To join route, take minor road from station. TL at TJ and follow road into Sampford Peverell. Take second TR and cross canal. TR at TJ, TL opposite church and follow road over A361. Join route at direction 6, where SO at XR, SP Huntsham/Bampton.

Starting from Tiverton, a gradual climb takes you along a beautiful valley to the town of Bampton. The route follows undulating quiet minor roads through Exebridge and beyond, giving glimpses of Exmoor, before the descent back to Tiverton, along a peaceful lane.

Places of interest along the route

A **Tiverton**

Tiverton was originally settled by the Saxons and was the wealthy centre of the wool trade between the 15th and 18th centuries. The **Grand Western Canal** was never fully completed and finally closed during the 1920s. A small stretch has been restored and horse-drawn barge trips are available April to September on varying days. Booking is advisable. Telephone (01884) 253345 for information. **Tiverton Castle** is over 900 years old and contains exhibitions on the Napoleonic Wars and civil war armoury, fine furniture and pictures. Also gardens. Open April to June and September, Sunday and Thursday, and Bank Holiday Mondays 1430–1730; July–August, Sunday–Thursday 1430–1730. Charge. Telephone (01844) 253200. **Tiverton Museum** was founded in 1960 and within its eight galleries displays a huge collection of exhibits on local history, including archaeology, cooking, toys and the railways. Museum shop. Open February to December, Monday–Saturday 1030–1630. Charge. Telephone (01884) 256295.

B **Bampton**

Bampton was also developed by the Saxons and followed Tiverton's prosperity in the wool trade. Today it is a quiet and attractive town. Bampton Castle no longer stands, but visitors can climb the site of the Norman castle for rewarding views.

Uplowman

Food and drink

There is lots of choice in Tiverton and Bampton.

Redwoods Inn, Uplowman
Skittle alley, bar meals and take away.

Jasmine Florist and Tearoom, Bampton
Wonderful tearoom in the back of a florist shop – enjoy a cup of tea and the scent of flowers. Closed Saturday afternoon and Sunday.

Anchor Inn, Exebridge
Lovely setting by the river, with picnic tables. Bar meals available.

Stag Inn, Rackenford
Twelfth-century pub, serving bar meals lunchtimes and evenings.

Rose and Crown, Calverleigh/ Tiverton
Outdoor picnic tables and umbrellas.

Route description

From the Tourist Information Centre, leave the car park and head uphill towards the town centre, passing distinctive high, bell-shaped street lights. TR at TJ, SP Hospital, and walk along the street. TR at end of street and walk 200m down one way street. Remount (next to statue of Edward the Peacemaker) and cross bridge.

1 TL along Blundell's Road, SP Cycle Route 3 (Sustrans SP).

2 TL onto dual carriageway, no SP.

3 SO at roundabout, SP Halberton.

4 TL along Uplowman Road, SP Uplowman. Cross bridge over A361.

5 TR at TJ, SP Uplowman/Huntsham (4.5km/ 3 miles), and cycle up quiet road with gradual gradient. Enter Uplowman.

6 If returning to Tiverton Parkway Station, TR at XR. Otherwise, TL at XR, SP Huntsham/ Bampton. Pass church on right. Cycle through this beautiful valley, beside stream on the left. Continue on this road, ignoring all turns, following SP Huntsham.

7 Arrive Huntsham (13km/8 miles). Bear right by the tree on a triangular intersection,

following SP Bampton, climbing a little harder now until reach top of hill and descend.

8 TL, SP Bampton and Unsuitable for Long Vehicles (18.5km/11.5 miles). Climb to top of hill for a fast descent into Bampton.

9 TR at TJ, Town Centre/Wiveliscombe. Cross bridge. **20km (12.5 miles)**

10 TR at TJ, SP Wiveliscombe B3227/ Morebath (B3190). Pass Tourist Information Centre on right.

11 TL, SP Morebath B3190.

12 TL, SP Exebridge/Dulverton. Cross old railway line and climb to top of hill for a fast descent and expansive view.

13 SO at XR, SP Brushford/Dulverton, then immediately TR, no SP (garage on right). Continue and cross bridge.

14 TL, SP Oldways End/South Molton (25.5km/16 miles). Follow this quiet, undulating road with one steep climb.

15 Pass under high power cables and TL, SP South Molton. **31.5km (19.5 miles)**

16 TL at TJ, no SP (SP Devon shortly after junction).

17 SO at XR across B3227, SP Rackenford.

18 TR (effectively SO) at Bickham Moor Cross, SP Knowstone. Descend. Cross cattle grid (35.5km/22 miles). Continue and cross bridge over A361.

19 TL at TJ, SP Rackenford. Cross cattle grid.

20 TL at TJ, SP Rackenford/ Tiverton. To visit Rackenford, TR, SP Rackenford, for 400m. Otherwise follow road round sharp bend to left (40km/25 miles). The road dips and climbs as you pass through Calverleigh and enter Tiverton.

21 TR at TJ into Kennedy Way, SP Bickleigh/Crediton/Halberton/Town Centre.

22 TL at XR, no SP, for 100m and cross bridge.

23 RHF uphill, into main street and TR, SP Tourist Information, to complete the route. **54km (33.5 miles)**

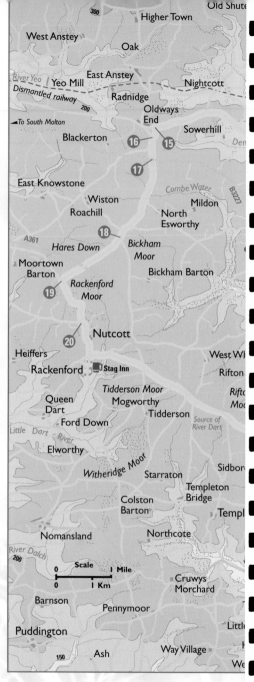

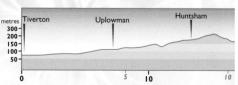

TINTAGEL AND THE NORTH CORNISH COAST

Route information

Distance 56.5km (35 miles)

Grade Moderate

Terrain Quiet back lanes dipping in and out of coastal harbours, lead to three steep climbs (which could be walked). The return is along mostly flat, tarmac roads.

Time to allow 4–8 hours.

Getting there by car Tintagel is on the north coast of Cornwall, north west of Camelford. It is signed from the A39. There are several car parks.

Getting there by train There is no practical railway access to this ride.

The north Cornish coast provides few havens for ships and it is into these few harbour villages that the outward leg of the route rises and falls. Starting at King Arthur's town of Tintagel, the coastal villages of Port Isaac and Port Quin are visited, followed by the beach resort of Polzeath (where the surfing is excellent). Inland for a gently undulating ride through St Endellion, St Teath and Delabole, the centre of the local slate industry. There is a viewing platform above the quarry, and also a windfarm with 11 huge windmills. The route continues to the British Cycling Museum at Old Camelford Station. Splendid views of the sea unfold as you descend back into Tintagel.

Places of interest along the route

A Tintagel

The town is best known for its connection to the legend of King Arthur. **Tintagel Castle** is the legendary birthplace of King Arthur. English Heritage maintain the remains of this 13th-century castle, once the stronghold of the Earls of Cornwall. To reach the castle, head out to Tintagel Head for 1km (0.6 mile). Open April to October, daily 1000–1800 (or dusk if earlier); November to March, daily 1000–1600. Charge. Telephone (01840) 770328. **King Arthur's Great Halls** were built in the 1930s by followers of the legend. Arthur's story is described in sound and music, and the atmosphere of King Arthur's court is brought to life. There are 72 stained glass windows, depicting the quest for the Holy Grail. Gift shop. Open all year, daily 1000–1700. Charge. Telephone (01840) 770526. **Tintagel Old Post Office** is a 14th-century manor house which was used as a post office during the 19th century. Fully restored and owned by the National Trust. Open April to October, daily 1100–1700. Telephone (01208) 74281.

B Longcross Victorian Gardens, near Port Isaac

Restored Victorian gardens feature granite and water features, maze and secret garden. Tearooms and tavern, serving lunchtime and evening meals. Gardens open all year, daily 1030–dusk. Tearooms/tavern open all year, 1030–2230. Charge for admission to gardens. Telephone (01208) 880243.

Food and drink

Plenty of opportunities for refreshment in Tintagel, Port Isaac and Delabole. There is a shop, pub, and fish and chip shop in Polzeath. Refreshments are also available at Portreath Bee Centre and Longcross Victorian Gardens.

Mill House Inn, Treknow
Open all day, serving cream teas.

Poldark Inn, near Westdowns
Good, basic bar meals.

White Hart, St Teath
Open all day, serving bar meals.

Ⓒ Portreath Bee Centre, near Polzeath

Visitors can clearly and safely watch bees in their colonies, making honey. Also gift shop, featuring honey and beeswax articles and Pooh Bear. Tearooms and picnic area. Bee exhibition open Easter to October, daily 1000–1700. Tearooms and shop open all year, daily 1000–1700. Charge for exhibition. Telephone (01208) 863718.

Ⓓ British Cycling Museum, Camelford

Britain's largest collection of cycling history grew from a hobby. The museum contains over 400 bicycles, old repair workshop, cycling medals, fobs and badges and a huge collection of other cycling memorabilia, dating from 1818. Open all year, Sunday–Thursday 1000–1700. Charge. Telephone (01840) 212811.

Tintagel Castle

Route description

Start at the Old Post Office in Tintagel, in the centre of town. With your back to the Post Office TR. TR again into Molesworth Street (just before the Methodist Church) SP Camelford B3263/Treknow/Trebarwith. Cycle along Molesworth Street and enter Treven. Pass Tintagel School on left. Enter Tregatta and pass SP Youth Hostel on sharp left hand bend.

1　TR, SP Treknow and descend steeply.

2　SO at XR, SP Trebarwith Village. Steep ascent and continue on this road.

3　TR at TJ, SP St Teath B3267/Port Isaac B3314 (6.5km/4 miles). Continue through Westdowns.

4　TR at XR, SP Port Gaverne. Follow road as it bends right and then left (10.5km/6.5 miles). Descend into Port Gaverne. Cycle down to bottom of hill, continue through village and climb out.

5　TR, no SP, down 16% hill. Pass SP Unsuitable for Caravans and continue down one way street (Back Hill), into Port Isaac.

6　TL at TJ opposite Old School Hotel, no SP. Descend to harbour, then climb steeply.

7　TR at TJ, SP Port Quin/Trelights, and Longcross Victorian Gardens on brown SP.

16km (10 miles)

8　To visit Longcross Victorian Gardens, TL for 50m. Entrance is on right. Otherwise, SO, SP Port Quin. Descend to bottom of hill (19km/ 12 miles) and then climb (not as steeply as previously). Continue through Port Quin.

9　TR at TJ (almost a XR), no SP (opposite direction is SP St Minver/Wadebridge/Bodmin). Pass Portreath Bee Centre on the right. Follow SP into centre of Polzeath (24.5km/15 miles). Climb out of Polzeath and through Trebetherick. Continue on road as it bears to left, SP St Minver/Wadebridge.

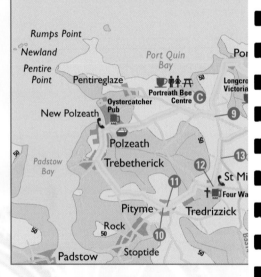

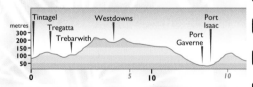

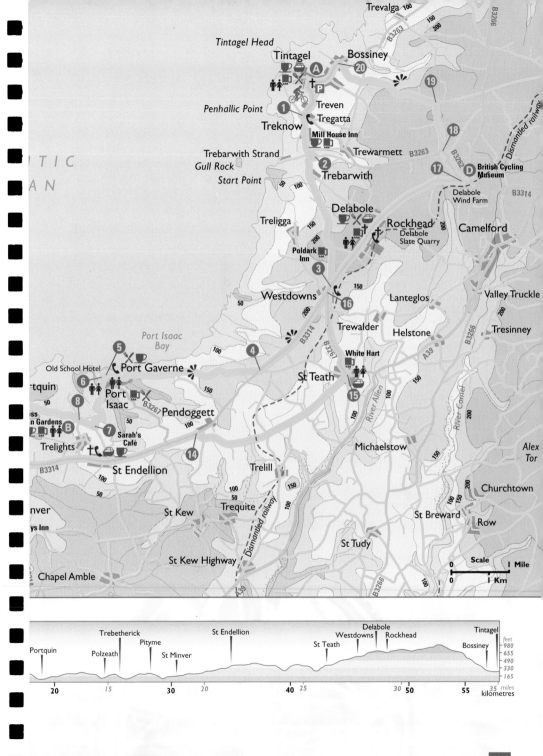

ATLANTIC OCEAN

Trevalga
Tintagel Head
Tintagel
Bossiney
Penhallic Point
Treven
Treknow
Tregatta
Mill House Inn
Trewarmett
Trebarwith Strand
Gull Rock
Start Point
Trebarwith
British Cycling Museum
Delabole Wind Farm
Treligga
Delabole
Rockhead
Camelford
Delabole Slate Quarry
Poldark Inn
Westdowns
Lanteglos
Valley Truckle
Trewalder
Helstone
Tresinney
Port Isaac Bay
White Hart
Old School Hotel
Port Gaverne
St Teath
Michaelstow
Alex Tor
tquin
Port Isaac
Pendoggett
Gardens
Sarah's Café
Trelights
St Endellion
Trelill
Churchtown
St Kew
Trequite
St Breward
Row
nver
ys Inn
St Kew Highway
St Tudy
Chapel Amble

Scale
0   1 Mile
0   1 Km

Elevation profile:

Portquin
Polzeath
Trebetherick
Pityme
St Minver
St Endellion
St Teath
Westdowns
Delabole
Rockhead
Bossiney
Tintagel

feet
980
655
490
330
165

20   15   30   20   40   25   30   50   55   35   miles
kilometres

10 TL at TJ, SP Wadebridge (B3314).

11 TL, SP St Minver. Continue through Tredrizzick. The road bends to right and enters St Minver. Pass church on right.

30.5km (19 miles)

12 TL at XR, SP Polzeath/Pendoggett. Pass cricket ground.

13 TL at TJ onto B3314, SP Delabole/Port Isaac. Follow road as it swings to right, SP Port Isaac/Trelights/St Endellion. Enter St Endellion (33.5km/21 miles) and continue through village. Pass church on left.

14 Just before SP Pendoggett, TR into narrow lane, SP St Teath (40km/25 miles). Continue towards St Teath as route goes under railway bridge, steeply down, climbs and passes under high power cables. Arrive St Teath.

15 TL at TJ, no SP (junction is at a clock tower, toilets opposite in pub car park. Cycle along North Road and under high power lines. Cross old railway.

16 TR at TJ onto B3314, SP Delabole. Enter Delabole (45km/28 miles). Continue through village and, further on, pass entrance to wind farm on right.

17 To visit British Cycling Museum, continue SO for 0.5km (0.3 mile). Otherwise, TL onto B3262, SP Trebarwith Strand/Tintagel (49.5km/31 miles). Continue on this road.

18 TR, SP Bossiney/Trevillett. Climb single track road and then descend, with Atlantic Ocean straight ahead.

19 TL at TJ, SP Bossiney/Tintagel/Trevillett. Pass stables on right and continue into Bossiney.

20 TL at TJ, onto B3263, SP Tintagel. Enter Tintagel. Pass church and Cornwall County Council car park on left and complete the route at the Old Post Office. *56.5km (35 miles)*

Tintagel Old Post Office

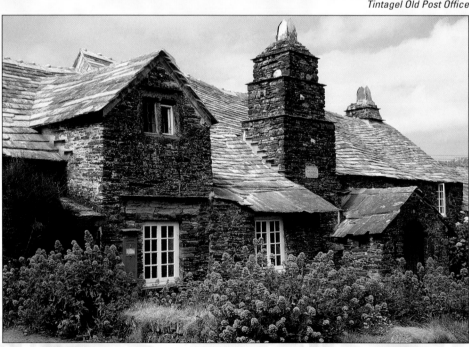

Route information

 Distance 59km (36.5 miles)

Grade Moderate

Terrain Quiet lanes throughout – a few hills but nothing too severe.

Time to allow 4–7 hours.

Getting there by car Bude is on the north Cornwall coast, close to the Devon border, on the A39. Follow SP for Town Centre and Visitor Information, where there is a long stay car park.

Getting there by train There is no practical railway access to this ride.

From the surfing town of Bude, out along the coast road to Widemouth Bay before making a circuit of narrow lanes, through pleasant farming country, to the small town of Holsworthy. From here quiet lanes take you to the Tamar Lakes, where there is a very pleasant tea stop. The route then heads west to Kilkhampton, before returning towards the sea.

Places of interest along the route

A Bude

A seaside town famous for its beaches and surf. The Bude Canal was originally developed to connect the Atlantic with the English Channel. However, construction only got as far as Launceston, 25.5km (16 miles) away, and after the arrival of the railway in Bude in 1898, the canal gradually fell into disuse. The start of the canal at Bude has been restored, providing access to the towpath and an abundance of wildlife. Telephone Bude Tourist Information Centre on (01288) 354240.

B Holsworthy

Holsworthy is a market town, dating from Saxon times, standing 6.5km (4 miles) from the Cornish border amid undeveloped countryside. The best day to visit is Wednesday, market day, when the town comes alive and visitors can enjoy the traditional country market. Holsworthy Tourist Information Centre can be contacted on (01409) 254185.

C Tamar Lakes, near Bude

The Tamar Lakes straddle the Cornwall and Devon border near the source of the River Tamar. There is plenty of birdlife and a bird hide on the Lower Lake, the quieter of the two lakes. The Upper Lake has a visitor and watersports centre. There are picnic spots on both lakes and a gift shop and tearoom on the Upper Lake. Visitor Centre, shop and tearoom open Easter to October, 1000–1700. Telephone (01288) 321712.

Food and drink

Refreshments are available in Bude, Widemouth Bay and Holsworthy. Kilkhampton and Poughill, each have a pub and a shop. There is a shop and two pubs in Week St Mary. However, the pubs should not be relied upon during the day, as they usually only open in the evening.

Café, Upper Tamar Lake
Indoor café serving good cyclists fare. Probably the best stop for cyclists on the route.

Route description

TL out of the Tourist Information Centre, no SP. Pass the Crescent Post Office and stores on right. Cross bridge and cycle along Vicarage Road, up hill and out of Bude. Continue through Upton, passing SP National Cycleway 3. Continue into Widemouth Bay, passing car park and beach entrance.

1 TL, SP Bideford/Wadebridge A39, into Leverlake Road. *4.5km (3 miles)*

2 SO at staggered XR, SP Week St Mary/ Bridgerule. Pass blue SP Unsuitable for Heavy Goods Vehicles and follow this narrow road as it curves to right.

3 TR at TJ, SP Week St Mary/Titson. Cross small bridge and cycle windy road, passing thatched farm house on left. *10.5km (6.5 miles)*

4 TL, no SP as such although there is small brown SP Cycle Route. Pass blue SP Unsuitable for Heavy Goods Vehicles on right. Descend into valley on narrow, grass-centred lane. Climb into Week St Mary.

5 TR at TJ, no SP, and continue into village centre. Pass Methodist Church on left (13.5km/8.5 miles) and continue, following SP for Launceston. Pass under high power cables.

6 TL, SP Launceston (B3254).

7 TL at XR, SP North Tamerton.

8 TL at TJ, SP Bude B3254/North Tamerton.

9 TR, SP North Tamerton (20km/12.5 miles). Pass Trepoyle Farm on left. Cycle into North Tamerton and continue SO through village and across bridge. *25.5km (16 miles)*

10 TR, SP Clawton (SP here is one sided, read from the other side). Cross weak bridge (SP as such). Enter Devon, SP on left, and cycle steadily uphill. Pass Affaland Farm on left. Keep on this lane towards Holsworthy.

11 LHF, no SP (32km/20 miles). Pass Chasty (house name) on left.

12 TL at TJ (Coles Mill Bridge), SP Town Centre/Bideford (A388)/Torrington (B3227). Climb hill into centre of town and pass under old railway bridge. Bear right towards church, following SP National Cycleway 3. Pass church on right.

13 TL, SP Bude (A3072), downhill, passing SP Sports Hall on right, and under metal pedestrian walkway.

14 TR, SP Chilsworthy/Bradworthy. Leave Holsworthy along a hedged road. Pass under high power cables. Enter Chilsworthy (36.5km/22.5 miles) on a bendy road with lots of turns.

15 TL, SP Pancrasweek.

16 TR at TJ, SP Sutcombe/Bradworthy. Then, within 100m, TL, SP Lana, along high hedged, single track lane. Follow road as it goes to right and continue.

17 TR at TJ (Gains Cross), SP Kilkhampton/Bradworthy. *41km (25.5 miles)*

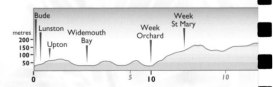

Widemouth Bay

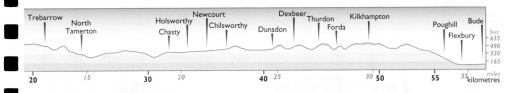

18 TL at TJ (Dunsdon Cross), SP Kilkhampton/Stratton.

19 TR, SP Dexbeer/Thurdon/Tamar Lakes, for a semi-steep descent. Continue to climb grass-centred road, high hedges on either side. Pass Lower Dexbeer Farm on right, then Higher Dexbeer Farm on left. Enter Cornwall and then the village of Thurdon.

20 To visit Tamar Lakes, TR, SP Upper Tamar Lake/Sutcombe (45km/28 miles). Follow this road for 1km (0.6 mile) and TL, SP Upper Tamar Lake. Otherwise, continue SO towards Kilkhampton.

21 TR at TJ, SP Kilkhampton/B3254, and continue into village.

22 TL at TJ, SP Bude A39/Stratton. Pass Kilkhampton Primary School on right.

23 TR, SP Stibb/Sandymouth/Coombe Valley (49.5km/31 miles). Continue through Stibb village.

24 TL, no SP (if miss this TL you will quickly pass SP Unsuitable for Heavy Goods Vehicles on left). Continue, with coastal views ahead.

25 TR at XR, SP Poughill, Bude (55.5km/34.5 miles). Continue through Ploughill, passing church on right. Follow road as it bends to left, SP Bude Town Centre, and pass church on left. Follow road as it swings left into one way system, SP golf club. Pass golf club on left and guest houses on right.

26 TR, SP Town Centre and shops. Immediately follow one way system to the left, down centre of Queen's Street.

27 TR at TJ, no SP, along the Strand, on the one way system. Pass Strand Hotel on left.

28 TR at TJ (at roundabout), SP Widemouth Bay (Coastal Route)/Toilets/Library/Tourist Information. Cross bridge and return to the Tourist Information Centre to complete the route. *59km (36.5 miles)*

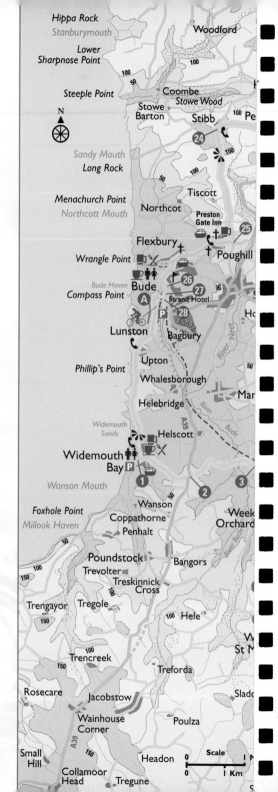

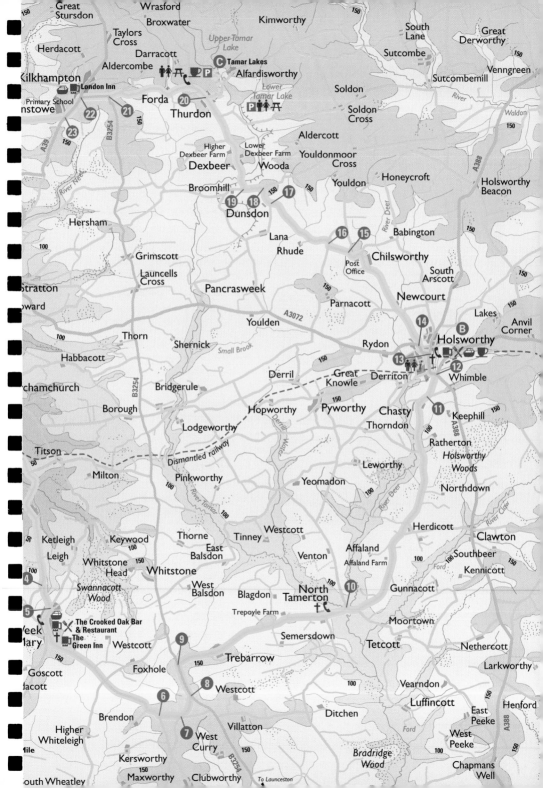

PENZANCE AND LAND'S END

Route information

 Distance 74.5km (46.5 miles)

Grade Moderate

Terrain A mixture of A and B roads and three off-road sections that can be tackled by a touring bicycle.

Time to allow 5–8 hours.

Getting there by car Penzance is on the A30. There are several long stay car parks in town – the most convenient is at the start of the route, by the railway station and Tourist Information Centre.

 Getting there by train There is a railway station in Penzance. Telephone (0345) 484950 for information.

From Penzance the route follows the coast westwards, with wonderful scenic views. On to Newlyn and Mousehole, which illustrate how important both the fishing and tourist industries are to this area. Inland now, as the road dips through the Lamorna Valley and on to Land's End. From here the route turns north, through St Just, where Cornwall's third great industry becomes increasingly apparent as old engine houses, reminders of the tin industry, regularly appear over the next 16km (10 miles). Three off-road sections follow, the third passing Carn Euny and providing a fabulous example of what life was like in Cornwall before tin, tourists and fishing fleets. A final descent takes you back into Newlyn and on to Penzance.

Places of interest along the route

A Penzance

The town's name comes from the Cornish for holy headland. Penzance was an isolated market town until the arrival of the railway, which not only increased trade but made the town a holiday centre. Today, it is a sunny, friendly town with a large harbour. **Trinity House National Lighthouse Centre**, at the harbour, has one of the largest collections of lighthouse equipment in the world. The exhibits include massive light optics, fog signals, navigation buoys and models of light vessels and ships. Also audio-visual presentation and replica lighthouse room. Gift shop. Open Easter to October, daily 1030–1630. Charge. Telephone (01736) 360077. **Penlee House Gallery and Museum** is surrounded by public park and holds the largest art collection in west Cornwall. The museum was founded in 1839 and the collection covers 6000 years of Cornish history, from the Stone Age to the present day. There is also a large photographic archive and image database, café and shop. Open all year, Monday–Saturday 1030–1630; also July and August, Sunday 1400–1630. Charge for entrance to art gallery and museum. Telephone (01736) 363625.

B Pilchard Works Museum, Newlyn

This award-winning museum, located in the busy fishing port of Newlyn, is also Britain's last working salt pilchard factory. Pilchards have been exported from here for over 90 years, and the museum describes a fascinating blend of social, artistic and industrial heritage. Visitors can see the factory in operation, taste the products and see many artefacts, paintings and photographs. Open Easter to November, Monday–Friday 1000–1800, Saturday 1000–1400. Charge. Telephone (01736) 332112.

C Land's End

The most westerly point of Britain. There is a conservation site, overlooking the Atlantic Ocean, where, during the summer, RSPB staff are on duty to answer visitors' questions. Also visitor centre with many attractions and displays, including the Land of Greeb, a 200-year-old Cornish Farm, the Last Labyrinth, an audio-visual experience of smugglers and ship-wreckers, and a theatre presentation on the local Air Sea Rescue Service. Various tea-rooms and gift shops and the Land's End Hotel. Open all year, daily 1000–1800. Admission to conservation site and visitor centre free, charge for attractions. Telephone (01736) 871220.

D Levant Beam Engine, near Pendeen

The oldest beam engine in Cornwall. The engine was built in 1840 to hoist ore from the Levant Mine. Now fully restored, visitors can experience the sights, sounds and smells of the working engine and view the mine shaft. Open Easter, May, Sunday–Monday and Bank Holidays; June, Wednesday–Friday and Sunday; July to October Sunday–Friday, 1000–1730. Charge. Telephone (01736) 786156.

E Geevor Tin Mine, near Pendeen

Visitors can tour the surface and underground at the largest preserved tin mine site in the UK. Also museum, film presentation and three-dimensional model of the underground workings. Gift shop and café. Open April to October, Sunday–Friday and Bank Holidays 1000–1730; November to March, Monday–Friday 1000–1600. Charge. Telephone (01736) 788662.

F Wayside Folk Museum, Zennor

Cornwall's oldest private museum provides a tranquil reminder of how life used to be. Until 1800 Zennor was so remote that all goods were transported by pack animals and sledges – there were no roads to the village. Against this background, a collection of ancient implements and customs was started which today comprises over 5000 items in 16 display areas, including a cobbler's shop, wheelwright's, 19th-century laundry room and miller's cottage. Also book shop and tearoom. Open April, daily 1100–1700; May to September, daily 1000–1800; October, Sunday–Friday 1100–1700. Charge. Telephone (01736) 796945.

G Carn Euny Settlement, near Sancreed

This settlement, founded by an early Cornish farming community, was inhabited between 500BC and 300AD. Discovered by Cornish tin miners, it contains the best preserved fogou (underground chamber) in Britain. The granite-lined 20m- (65 feet-) long underground passage leads to a circular chamber which may have been used for purposes of religion, storage or habitation. Access at all reasonable times. Admission free. For further information telephone Penzance Tourist Information Centre on (01736) 362207.

Food and drink

Lots of choice for refreshments in Penzance, Mousehole, Sennen and St Just. Also pubs/cafés in St Buryan, Pendeen, Zennor, Newbridge and at Land's End Aerodrome. Refreshments are also available at Penlee House Gallery and Museum, Land's End, Geevor Tin Mine and the Wayside Folk Museum.

Lamorna Wink, near Lamorna Cove

This pub got its curious name from the custom of selling something stronger than beer from under the counter, when it was licensed to sell only beer.

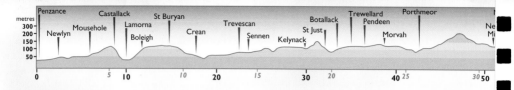

Route description

From the car park by the railway station and Tourist Information Centre, follow the one way system, SP Newlyn/Mousehole/Land's End. Pass the National Lighthouse Museum on right and SO at roundabout, SP Newlyn/Mousehole. Bear left, following SP Mousehole and pass Newlyn Harbour on left. To visit the Pilchard Works TR into The Coombe, opposite North Pier. Continue on to and through Mousehole. Climb out of village and follow SP Lamorna.

1 TL at TJ, SP Lamorna via Castallack (7.5km/5 miles). Descend into Lamorna.

2 TR at TJ, SP Penzance/Land's End (10km/ 6 miles). The Lamorna Wink pub is TL at this junction.

3 TL at TJ, SP Land's End/Porthcurno/St Buryan.

4 TR, SP St Buryan.

5 TL at TJ, SP Logan Rock/Porthcurno/ Land's End. *15km (9.5 miles)*

6 TR, SP Crean. Descend then climb out of valley.

7 TR at TJ, SP Land's End. *19.5km (12 miles)*

8 To visit Land's End, TL at TJ, SP Land's End. Otherwise, TR at TJ, SP Penzance/Sennen. Continue through Sennen.

9 TL onto B3306, SP St Just (26.5km/ 16.5 miles). Continue towards St Just.

10 TL at TJ, SP St Just/Zennor (31.5km/ 19.5 miles). Cycle through St Just and continue on B3306 as it winds through small settlements. Pass Levant Beam Engine and then Geevor Tin Mine on left (35.5km/22 miles). Continue through Pendeen and stay on this road (B3306) towards Zennor.

11 To visit Zennor and the Wayside Folk Museum, SO for 1km (0.6 mile). Otherwise, TR, SP Newmill/Penzance. *45.5km (28.5 miles)*

12 TL at TJ, SP Gulval/Penzance.

13 TR, SP Trythall/Tredinnick/Bodrifty/Ding Dong. *50.5km (31.5 miles)*

14 TR, SP Tredinnick/Bodrifty. Follow road as it swings left and climbs. When old engine house appears close to road on right, take grassy track to right. Continue past houses on right and follow well-defined track, passing mine shaft warning SP. Continue on track as it swings left in front of another engine house to rejoin tarmac next to Bosiliack Farm.

15 TL at TJ (effectively SO).

16 TR, SP Newbridge.

17 TR at TJ onto A3071, SP St Just/ Newbridge (56km/35 miles). Pass Jericho Farm on right and shortly after:

18 TL onto bridleway, partially tarmacked, as it descends past farm on right and finishes by crossing a ford.

19 TR at TJ, no SP. *61km (38 miles)*

20 TR at TJ, SP St Just. Then TL onto track next to brick pointed arch. Follow track uphill – it flattens to pass Carn Euny settlement on left. Descend through farm and back onto tarmac.

21 TL (effectively SO), SP Sancreed. *66km (41 miles)*

22 TR at TJ, SP Drift/Penzance.

23 SO at XR, SP Chyenhal.

24 TL at TJ, SP Penzance. *70.5km (44 miles)*

25 SO at XR, SP Penzance. Continue back into Penzance, following SP Station/Tourist Information, and complete the route. *74.5km (46.5 miles)*

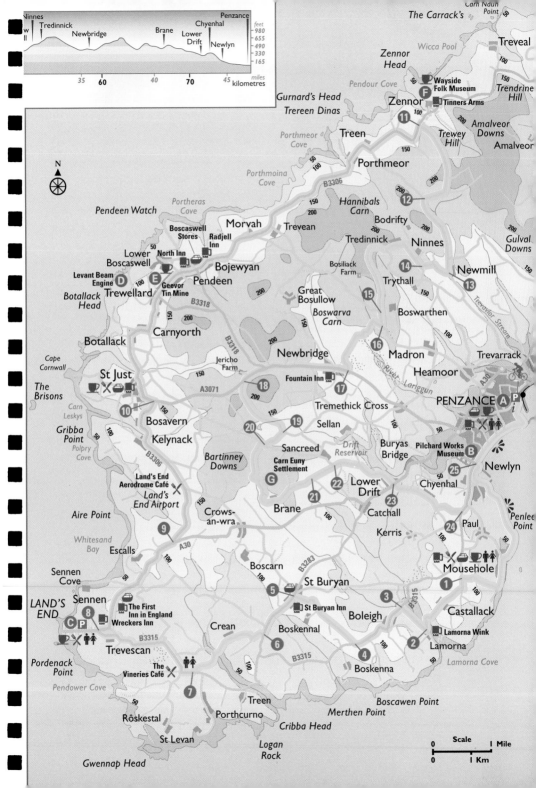

BARNSTAPLE AND THE TARKA TRAIL

Distance 78km (48.5 miles)

Grade Outward strenuous, return easy.

Terrain Rolling, narrow, hedged lanes with little traffic and a number of short steep climbs. The route ends with an easy return along the well-surfaced, traffic-free Tarka Trail.

Time to allow 4–8 hours.

Getting there by car Barnstaple is at the end of the A361 north Devon link road, signed from the M5. There are several car parks in the town. The most convenient is a pay and display car park by the railway station.

Getting there by train Barnstaple is the final stop on the Tarka Line from Exeter. Telephone (0345) 484950 for information.

The obvious route taken by so many is to cycle both ways along the Tarka Trail. This route provides a chance to explore a part of north Devon now bypassed by so many since the opening of the traffic-free Tarka Trail. The outward route is hilly in places, as you pass through Tawstock, Torrington, and the beautiful valley around Weare Gifford. The return is along the Tarka Trail.

Places of interest along the route

A Museum of North Devon, Barnstaple

The museum contains many fascinating exhibits illustrating north Devon, its people and landscape. Displays cover subjects from Iron Age Devon and prehistoric animals through to a replica Wellington aircraft and Tarka the Otter, whose life was described by Henry Williamson. Shop and tearoom. Open all year, Tuesday–Friday 1000–1630, Saturday 1000–1630. Charge. Telephone (01271) 346747.

B Dartington Crystal, Great Torrington

Factory tours and visitor centre with permanent exhibition of glassmaking and engraving. Also factory and kitchenware shop, mill shop and restaurant. Site open all year, Monday–Saturday 0930–1700, Sunday 1030–1630. Factory tours available Monday–Friday 0930–1600. Charge for tours. Telephone (01805) 626266.

C Rosemoor Garden, Great Torrington

Run by the Royal Horticultural Society, Rosemoor covers 16ha (40 acres) and contains colour themed gardens, herbs and potager, herbaceous borders, cottage, winter and fruit and vegetable gardens. Also arboretum, stream and bog gardens. Visitor centre with shop and restaurant. Open all year, April to September, daily 1000–1800; October to March, daily 1000–1700. Charge for admission to gardens. Telephone (01805) 624067.

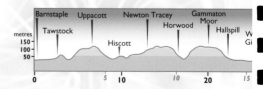

Landcross Aqueduct, River Torridge

D Barometer World and Museum, Merton

Devon once had over 30 barometer makers. Barometer World creates and restores these intriguing instruments. Also on the site is a collection of barometers and an exhibition illustrating their workings and development from circa 1680 to the present day. Open February to December, Monday–Saturday 0900–1700, although visitors should telephone to confirm opening times on (01805) 603443. Charge for exhibition.

E Tarka Trail

Traffic-free track offering miles of cycling and named after *Tarka the Otter* by Henry Williamson. The flat, well-surfaced track follows the line of the now disused Southern Railway, following the River Torridge through rural Devon and along the coast by the River Taw to Barnstaple. The Tarka Trail is open all year, at all reasonable times. There are many items of interest along the trail, including Instow Signal Box, saved from demolition and fully restored. Open all year, Sunday and Bank Holidays 1400–1700. For further information on the trail, telephone (01837) 83399.

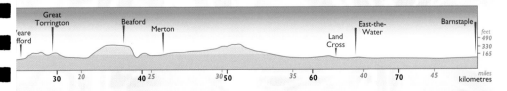

Route description

From Barnstaple railway station, leave the car park and TL at mini roundabout. Follow cycle track past B&Q on left, until you arrive at roundabout where TL and cycle up hill.

1 TL, SP Lake/Tawstock, and climb. Cross bridge and then pass under another bridge. Enter Tawstock and pass thatched school on right.

2 TL, SP Collabear (4.5km/3 miles). Cycle along flat valley floor, passing turn to Newton Tracey on right.

3 TR at TJ (opposite farm at Uppacott), no SP.

4 TL at TJ, SP Hiscott/Harracott.

5 TR at XR, SP Hiscott/Harracott, and enter Harracott.

6 TR at TJ, SP Hiscott/Newton Tracey. Continue into Hiscott.

7 TR, no SP, in centre of Hiscott.
10km (6 miles)

8 TL at TJ, no SP. Pass East Pristacott Farm on left. Continue into Newton Tracey.

9 TR at TJ, SP Barnstaple/B3232.

10 TL, SP Lovacott/Horwood. Enter Horwood.

11 TL, SP Ashridge/Torrington (16km/ 10 miles). Cycle through wooded valley.

12 SO at XR (Webbery Cross), SP Gammaton Moor/Torrington.

13 SO at XR, no SP (SP is twisted here, away from direction). Pass SP Weight Limit on right.
20km (12.5 miles)

14 TR, SP Weare Giffard/Cheese Store.

15 TR, SP Hallspill, for a steep descent down narrow road – take care.

16 TL at TJ, SP Torrington. Pass church on right and cycle through Weare Giffard (25.5km/ 16 miles). Continue to cross stream and climb. Pass Torrington Golf Club on right then right turn to Dartington Crystal.

17 TL at TJ, SP Okehampton A386/South Molton/Exeter. TR into Potacre Street, no SP. TL at XR into Well Street, SP Exeter/Plymouth.

18 TR at XR, no SP.　　*30.5km (19 miles)*

19 TL, SP Winkleigh/Exeter B3220/Beaford. Pass entrance to Rosemoor Garden and continue on this road into Beaford.　*39km (24 miles)*

20 TR into Green Lane, SP Beaford Centre. Descend, with view of Dartmoor on left, and cross bridge at bottom of hill.

21 TL, SP Merton. Follow road as it bends to right and continue into Merton. Pass Barometer World on left.

22 TL at TJ, no SP.　　*44km (27.5 miles)*

23 TR, SP Petrockstow/Shebbear/Tarka Trail.

24 Entrance to Tarka Trail on left (46.5km/29 miles). Follow the well-graded trail along the old railway line, passing Tarka Trail Information Centre (64.5km/40 miles). Continue to Barnstaple and the end of the railway section of cycle trail. TR and return to railway station and end of route.　*78km (48.5 miles)*

Food and drink

There are many places offering refreshment in Barnstaple and Great Torrington, pubs in Beaford and Merton, as well as tearooms at Bideford and Instow, along the Tarka Trail. Refreshments are also available at the Museum of North Devon, Dartington Crystal and Rosemoor Garden.

Hunters Inn, Newton Tracey
Bar meals served.

Cider Press, Weare Giffard
Free house serving meals.

TRURO AND THE ROSELAND PENINSULA

Route information

🚲 **Distance** 79km (49 miles)

🚲 **Grade** Strenuous

🚲 **Terrain** Tarmac roads throughout. There are a number of steep climbs and descents on the outward section of the route.

🚲 **Time to allow** 5–9 hours.

🚲 **Getting there by car** Truro is reached via the A39. There are several long stay car parks in the town.

🚲 **Getting there by train** Truro is on the main line into Cornwall. Telephone (0345) 484950 for information.

Starting from Truro, the ride heads south to the King Harry ferry crossing over the River Fal. From here a section of quiet B road and busier A road takes you into the challenging, but scenically rewarding, section of the ride, as you descend and climb out of the delightful villages and harbours around the Roseland Peninsula. The route continues through the popular holiday centres of Mevagissey and Pentewan, before winding its way back to Truro along a series of mostly quiet lanes. For information on the ferry, telephone Truro Tourist Information Centre on (01872) 274555.

Places of interest along the route

A Truro
There has been a settlement on this site for thousands of years, but it was the advent of copper and tin mining, and the town's status as a port, that brought wealth to Truro. During the 18th century, Truro was a fashionable Georgian town and by the mid-19th century had grown into an industrial centre. Today Truro is the administrative centre of Cornwall. For further information, telephone Truro Tourist Information Centre on (01872) 274555.

B Trelissick Gardens, Feock
Tranquil gardens with wonderful maritime views down Carrick Road to the open sea. Parkland and riverside woods. Also gallery displaying local art and crafts, shop and restaurant. National Trust property. Open March to October, Monday–Saturday 1030–1730, Sunday 1230–1730. Charge. Telephone (01872) 862090.

C The Lost Gardens of Heligan, Pentewan
The gardens of Heligan lay hidden under brambles for over 70 years before restoration began in 1991. Now over 32ha (80 acres) of garden have been reclaimed and restored, and include spectacular tree ferns, bamboo and tropical vegetation, a walled garden, hothouses and ponds. Plant sales and tearoom. Open all year, daily 1000–1800. Charge. Telephone (01726) 844157.

D Trewithen Gardens, near Truro
The 12ha (30 acres) of gardens contain magnificent collections of camellias, rhododrendrons and magnolias. Plant sales and tearoom. Open March to September, Monday–Saturday 1000–1630; also April and May, Sunday 1000–1630. Charge. Telephone (01726) 883647.

Route description

TL out of Tourist Information Centre in Princess Street. Then, almost immediately, TL into Lemon Street, and walk along one way street. After 100m, where traffic becomes two way, carry SO, passing Conservative Club on right and pillared memorial on left. SO at large round-about, SP Falmouth. TL immediately, into Old Falmouth Road. Descend to cross bridge and follow road uphill, SP Kea School. Pass school.

1 TL into Carlyon Road, then TR into Penhalls Way.

2 TL at TJ, into Holywell Road.

3 TL at TJ, no SP, and continue through Penelewey.

4 TL at XR, SP King Harry Ferry (6.5km/4 miles). Pass Trelissick Gardens on right. Arrive at King Harry Ferry (8.5km/5 miles) and cross River Fal. On other side, continue on B3289.

5 Arrive St Just in Roseland and TL at TJ, no SP. Continue on A3078, through Trewithian.

6 TR, SP Veryan/Portloe/Portholland (21km/13 miles). Enter Veryan.

7 SO at XR, no SP. Then TR at TJ, past store on right.

8 SO at XR, SP Camels/Portloe (24km/15 miles). Enter Portloe and climb out of the village and into Treviskey.

9 TR, SP Portholland. Pass Veryan Vineyard on right and continue on a steep, wooded descent.

10 TR at TJ, SP Portholland. Descend into village.

11 TL at TJ, no SP. *29.5km (18.5 miles)*

12 TR at TJ, SP Caerhays/Gorran Haven. Continue past Porthluney Beach (34.5km/21.5 miles) and into Tregavarras.

13 TR, SP Boswinger/Hemmick. Pass through Boswinger to descend and climb steeply.

14 TR, no SP (as road bears left, opposite wooden gate with SP Footpath to Treveague). Cycle along this beautiful gated cliffside road and descend into Gorran Haven.

15 TL at TJ, into Rice Lane. For shops, café and WC, TR at TJ (41km/25.5 miles). Follow road as it climbs out of village and becomes Bell Hill.

16 SO at XR. Pass unsuitable for motors sign, then TR at TJ, no SP. Continue, following SP Portmellon. Descend into Mevagissey, follow one way system past car parks and climb out of village, along B3273. To visit Heligan, TL and follow road for 2km (1 mile). Otherwise, continue past Pentewan Beach and into London Apprentice.

17 TL, SP Polgooth. *53km (33 miles)*

18 TL, SP Sticker/St Ewe.

19 SO at XR, SP Hewas Water.

Food and drink

There are plenty of opportunities for refreshment in Truro and also pubs/ tearooms in Penelewey, Veryan, Portloe, Porthluney Beach, Gorran Haven, Mevagissey, Grampound and Probus.

There are convenience stores along the route. Refreshments are also available at Trelissick, Heligan and Trewithen gardens.

Melinsey Mill, near Veryan
Tearoom in a reconstructed water mill in lovely surroundings. Tours of the mill, and tea and cakes by the mill pond.

20 TL at TJ, SP St Austell/Truro.
57km (35.5 miles)

21 TL at TJ onto A390 for 50m, SP Truro.
Then TL, SP Tregony/St Mawes.

22 TR at TJ, SP Tregony/St Mawes.

23 TR at TJ, SP Grampound/Truro.
60.5km (37.5 miles)

24 TL, SP Creed.

25 TR, no SP. Pass Trewarmenna Farm on
right.

26 TL at TJ onto A390, no SP, and continue
into Grampound. Take care on this road.

27 TL, SP Bartliver/Golden Mill, back onto a
narrow lane.

28 TL at TJ, SP Tregony/St Mawes. Pass
entrance to Trewithen Gardens on right.
65km (40.5 miles)

29 TR at XR, SP Probus.

30 TR at TJ onto A390, SP Probus.

31 TL at roundabout, SP Probus. SO at mini
roundabout, passing church on left.

32 TR at TJ onto A390, SP Truro (71km/
44 miles). Enter Tresillian.

33 TL, SP Pencalenick, and continue into
Truro.

34 SO at roundabout, SP Perranporth. Then
TL by car park into Old Bridge Street. At TJ,
walk right and take Cathedral Lane back to
Tourist Information Centre and the end of the
route. **79km (49 miles)**

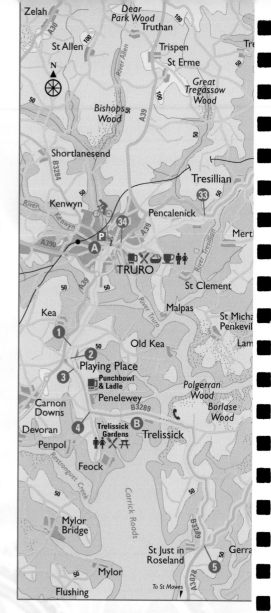

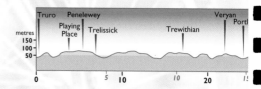

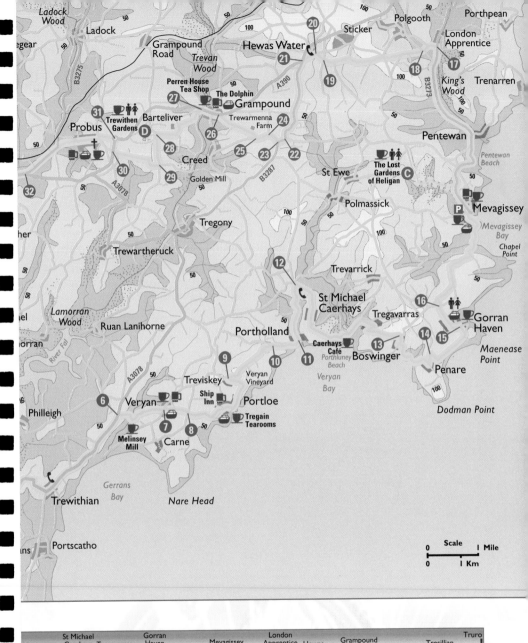

Ladock Wood
Ladock
egear
Grampound Road
Trevan Wood
20 Hewas Water
21
Sticker
Polgooth
Porthpean
London Apprentice
17
18
King's Wood
Trenarren
19
B3275
A390
Perren House Tea Shop
27
The Dolphin
Grampound
31 Trewithen Gardens
Barteliver
Probus
D
Trewarmenna Farm
26
24
B3273
Pentewan
28
Creed
25 **23** **22**
St Ewe
The Lost Gardens of Heligan
C
Pentewan Beach
30
29
Golden Mill
A3078
B3287
Polmassick
P Mevagissey
32
100
Mevagissey Bay
Tregony
Chapel Point
her
Trewartheruck
Trevarrick
Lamorran Wood
12
St Michael Caerhays
16
Ruan Lanihorne
Tregavarras
Gorran Haven
orran
River Fal
Portholland
9
10
Caerhays Café
Parthluney Beach
11
13 Boswinger
14 **15**
Maenease Point
A3078
Treviskey
Veryan Vineyard
Veryan Bay
Penare
6 Veryan
Ship Inn
Portloe
Philleigh
7
8
Tregain Tearooms
Dodman Point
Melinsey Mill
Carne
Trewithian
Gerrans Bay
Nare Head
Portscatho
ns

Scale
0   1 Mile
0   1 Km

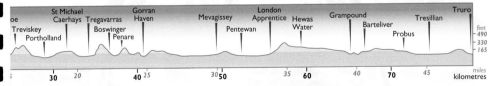

oe
Treviskey
Portholland
St Michael Caerhays
Tregavarras
Boswinger
Penare
Gorran Haven
Mevagissey
Pentewan
London Apprentice
Hewas Water
Grampound
Barteliver
Probus
Tresillian
Truro

feet
490
330
165

30   20   40 25   30 50   35   60   40   70   45

miles
kilometres

89

SOUTH MOLTON TO EXMOOR

Route information

Distance 86km (53.5 miles)

Grade Moderate

Terrain Good quality roads, a stretch of A road and a few steep climbs.

Time to allow 5–10 hours.

Getting there by car South Molton is in north Devon, close to the A361 Barnstaple road. Long stay car parking is available near the town centre.

Getting there by train There is no railway station at South Molton. However, the route can be accessed by taking the Tarka Line from Exeter to King's Nympton, where TR out of station onto A377 (see direction 1) and continue.

A classic day ride for an experienced cyclist. A quick, flat stretch of A and B road winds its way from South Molton along an attractive valley floor to Eggesford. From here, a gradual climb along quiet roads takes you towards the western edge of Exmoor, with the conveniently placed Moortown Diner en route. The final section of the route is on one of the prettiest roads in the West Country, as you follow the Devon border with extensive views to the west. A final swoop into South Molton ends the route.

Places of interest along the route

Ⓐ South Molton Museum, South Molton
Local history museum illustrating the life and times of South Molton and the surrounding district through photographs, documents and many fascinating exhibits. Open March to November, Monday, Tuesday and Thursday 1030–1300 and 1400–1600, Wednesday and Saturday 1030–1230. Admission free. Telephone (01769) 572951.

Ⓑ Hancocks Devon Cider, South Molton
Devon scrumpy is made here, in the traditional manner. Visitors can visit the mill and see how the cider is made. Also farm shop and café. Open Easter to September, Monday–Saturday 0900–1300 and 1400–1700. Charge. Telephone (01769) 572678.

Ⓒ Eggesford Garden Centre, Eggesford
Garden centre with restaurant and coffee shop, visitor centre, picnic areas, off-road cycle trails and forest walks. Also cycle hire. Open all year, daily 0900–1800. Admission free. Telephone (01769) 580250.

Ⓓ Quince Honey Farm, South Molton
A living honey bee exhibition. Visitors can safely watch the bee colonies from behind glass. Also farm shop and tearoom. Open Easter to September, daily 0900–1800; October 0900–1700. Charge for exhibition. Telephone (01769) 572401.

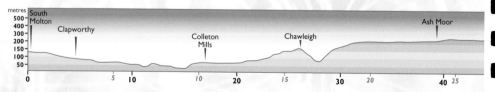

Route description

Start in the centre of South Molton, with Guildhall on left, and leave town bearing left along B3226. Pass Hancocks Devon Cider on left (4.5km/3 miles) and continue on this valley road. Cross river.

1 TL at TJ, SP Exeter A377 (14.5km/9 miles). Pass King's Nympton Station on right. Enter Eggesford (21km/13 miles). Pass Eggesford Station on right.

2 To visit Eggesford Garden Centre, TR just after station, SP Wembworthy/Winkleigh and take first TL. TL SP Chawleigh/Witheridge/B3042. Cycle uphill and pass Pheasant Tree Farm on right. Follow road as it swings to right, SP B3042/ Chawleigh/Witheridge, and continue into Chawleigh. **_25km (15.5 miles)_**

3 TL beside Earl of Portsmouth pub (Portsmouth Arms Cross), SP Cheldon/Gidleigh Arms. Descend quite steeply and follow road round to left, SP Gidleigh Arms, for a steep climb (25%).

4 TR at TJ (Stone Moor Cross), SP Witheridge/Worlington (29.5km/18.5 miles). Continue along wide, flattish, quiet road, following SP Witheridge.

5 SO at XR (Burrow Cross), SP Witheridge/Knowstone/South Molton.

6 SO at XR, across B3137, SP Knowstone (35.5km/22 miles). Pass lots of satellite dishes on left and continue through Ash Moor.

7 SO at XR (Batsworthy Cross), SP Knowstone/Tiverton. **_40.5km (25 miles)_**

8 TR at TJ (Beaple's Moor Cross), SP Knowstone/Tiverton. Pass Moortown Diner on right.

Exmoor

9 TR at TJ, SP Tiverton/Taunton/Exeter/Knowlstone. Immediately TL SP Knowstone/Mason's Arms Inn. Cross cattle grid and enter Roachill. **_44.5km (27.5 miles)_**

10 TR at TJ, SP Bampton B3227. Immediately TL, SP East Anstey.

11 TL at TJ (Tuckers Moor Cross), SP East Anstey/Dulverton. Follow SP East Anstey. Pass Methodist Church on right and New Park Farms on left.

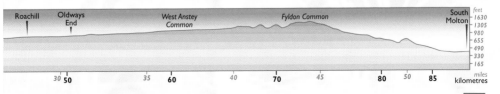

12 TR, SP Hawkridge/Tarr Steps (49.5km/ 31 miles). Continue on winding road, steadily climbing towards Exmoor.

13 TL at TJ, SP Hawkridge/Molland. Follow SP National Cycle Route 3. Enter National Park. Cross cattle grid (55.5km/34.5 miles). Cycle through open moorland. Pass memorial stone on right, then cattle grid.

14 TR at XR, SP Hawkridge/Withypool (61km/ 38 miles). Follow SP National Cycle Route 3.

15 TL at XR, and cross cattle grid, SP Sandyway/Withypool. (This is a difficult junction as five roads meet in the same place – be sure to cross cattle grid.)

16 TR at XR (Mudgate Cross), SP Withy-pool/Sandyway.

17 TR at TJ (Sandyway Cross), SP Withypool/Simonsbath (65km/40.5 miles). Then, TL, SP Simonsbath/Route 3.

18 TL at XR (Kinsford Gate Cross), SP Brayford/South Molton (72.5km/45 miles). Steep descent before road flattens out.

19 TL at TJ, SP South Molton A399/(B3226).
81.5km (50.5 miles)

20 SO at roundabout, SP South Molton. Continue into South Molton, passing Quince Honey Farm on right, and complete the route.
86km (53.5 miles)

Food and drink

There is plenty of choice in South Molton and a couple of pubs in Chawleigh. Refreshments are also available at Hancocks Devon Cider, Quince Honey Farm and Eggesford Garden Centre.

Moortown Diner, Moortown
Small café serving good basic food.

Sportsmans Arms, near Sandy Way
Real ale and restaurant meals.

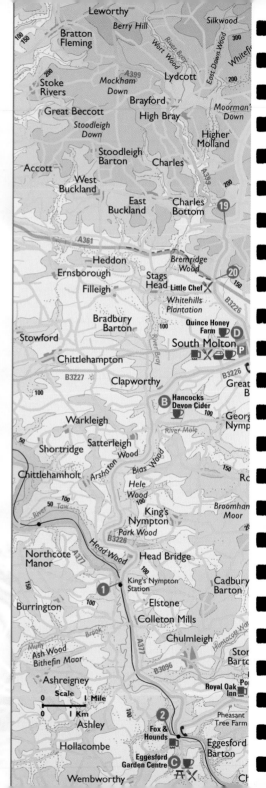

SOUTH HAMS AND THE PLYM VALLEY

Route information

 Distance 88.5km (55 miles)

Grade Strenuous

Terrain A variety of A and B roads and lanes. One long off-road section on a reasonably well-surfaced cycle trail. Some steep ascents.

Time to allow 5–10 hours.

Getting there by car Ivybridge is on the A38 Exeter to Plymouth road. There is a long stay car park at the Tourist Information Centre.

Getting there by train There is a station on the outskirts of Ivybridge. Telephone (0345) 484950 for information.

From Ivybridge, the route heads east to Bittaford before following a series of quiet, narrow lanes around the hamlet of Owley. On to South Brent and through some of the lovely villages and towns of the South Hams area of Devon, eventually arriving at the yachting village of Newton Ferrers. The route then heads north, to meet the Plym Valley Cycle Trail, a traffic-free, dedicated cycle route. The final stretch of the route skirts the south side of Dartmoor, through Cornwood, before returning to Ivybridge. The route goes through a dark tunnel along the cycle track – bicycle lights are advisable.

Places of interest along the route

Ⓐ Modbury

This attractive Devon town, full of 18th- and early 19th-century houses, was once an important agricultural centre – there were at one time ten pubs in the town. Of the two remaining, the Exeter Inn is a striking example of a half-timbered building.

Ⓑ Newton Ferrers

One of the area's most popular and picturesque yachting harbours. The village's name comes from the Norman Henry de Ferriers, who owned the village after the Norman Conquest.

Ⓒ Saltram House, near Underwood

A magnificent George II mansion, featured in the film *Sense and Sensibility*, and set in landscaped parkland overlooking the River Plym. The house contains plasterwork by Robert Adam and a Georgian collection of paintings, including ten by Sir Joshua Reynolds. Visitors can also see the Great Kitchen, the orangery and an exhibition of local art in the chapel. Gift shop and tearoom. National Trust property. House and garden open April to September, Sunday–Thursday and Bank Holidays 1230–1730 (open 1130 on Sunday and Bank Holidays); October and November, Sunday–Thursday 1230–1630. Garden also open March, weekends only 1100–1600. Charge. Telephone (01752) 336546.

South Devon village

Route description

Leave car park at Tourist Information Centre, across speed bumps. Pass through other long stay car park and TL at TJ, opposite Police Station. Immediately TL at roundabout, SP Bittaford/Ugborough. Cross zebra crossing and TR at roundabout (opposite Bridge Inn) onto B3213, SP Bittaford/Ugborough. Leave Ivybridge, passing railway station entrance. To join the route from here, TL out of the station onto B3213 to direction 1.

1 TL into Wrangaton Road and under railway viaduct. Climb, passing post office on left.

2 TL at Shute Cross, SP Owley, into a narrow lane (6km/3.5 miles). Continue through Owley, passing Owley Farm on right.

3 TL at TJ, no SP. Pass cream coloured houses on right and TR at TJ, SP Brent. Cross bridge over waterfall. Enter South Brent. Bear left along Station Approach, parallel to railway on right.

4 TR at TJ, SP South Brent/Plymouth, and cross railway line.

5 TL at TJ, into Fore Street. **11km (7 miles)**

6 TR at TJ, SP Plymouth (A38)/Avonwick (B3210).

7 TL, SP Avonwick/Totnes. Immediately TR and pass behind Woodpecker Inn. Climb up this narrow lane.

8 TL at TJ onto A3121 (effectively SO), no SP.

9 TR, no SP (15km/9.5 miles). Continue into and through Ugborough, passing church on left.

10 SO at XR (Haredon Cross), no SP.

11 TR at TJ (Dunwell Cross), SP Modbury.

12 TL opposite Ludbrook Manor, no SP.
 21km (13 miles)

13 TL at TJ at Sheepham Bridge. Cross bridge and climb steeply into Modbury.

14 TR at TJ, into Barrocks Road.

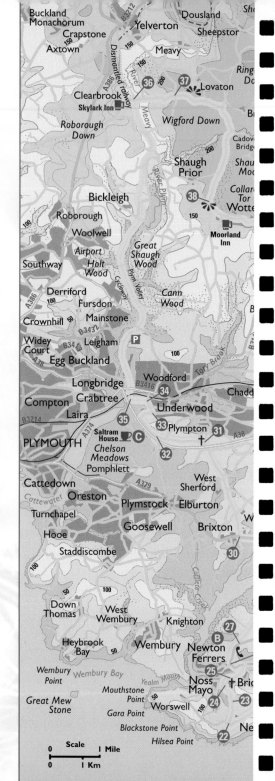

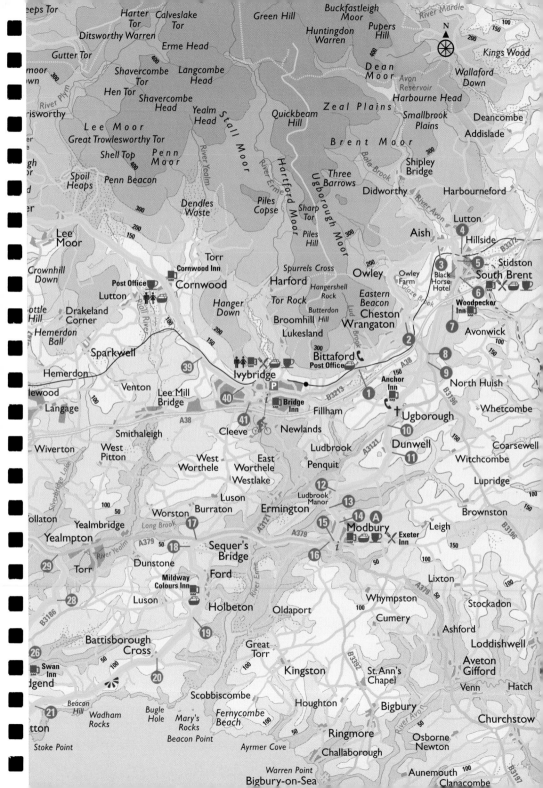

15 TL at TJ at Palm Cross. Follow road as it descends into centre of Modbury. TR at XR just past zebra crossing, SP Tourist Information/ Health Centre. Cycle along Poundwell Street and pass Tourist Information on left. Continue along steep, hedged lane. TR into Church Lane.

24km (15 miles)

16 TL at TJ onto A379, no SP.

17 TL, SP Holbeton.

18 TL, SP Ford, and continue into Ford. At foot of village, bear right and climb steeply. Continue through Holbeton.

19 SO at XR (White Moor Cross), SP Battisborough/Mothercombe/Alston (31.5km/ 19.5 miles). Follow SP Battisborough/ Mother-combe/Alston and bear right at Hembury Cross.

20 SO at XR (Battisborough Cross) and follow SP Newton Ferrers.

21 SO at XR (Stoke Cross), SP Netton/ Worswell. *39.5km (24.5 miles)*

22 TR (at Langdon Hill), SP Netton/Noss Mayo.

23 TL, no SP, along tree-lined alleyway.

24 TR at TJ, then immediately TL at TJ (opposite Yonder Coombe house). Descend for 50m and TR just before church. Pass Melody Cottage and then Methodist Church on right.

25 TL at TJ (effectively SO), no SP. Follow road round to the left, SP Newton Ferrers Plymouth. Lovely view to left, back along estuary. Climb and leave Newton Ferrers.

26 TR at TJ at green, no SP (telephone on right).

27 TL just in front of water tower, no SP.

28 TL at TJ, no SP (45km/28 miles), and descend to foot of valley. Cross bridge.

29 TL at TJ onto A379, SP Brixton/ Plymouth.

30 TR up Red Lion Hill (just before church and school), SP Plympton. Pass under A38.

50km (31 miles)

31 TL, SP The Gables.

32 TR at TJ, no SP (crash barriers on left) onto road parallel to A38 (55km/34 miles). Follow road as it swings right and passes Saltram House on left. *55km (34 miles)*

33 TL down Cot Hill, SP Plympton/City Centre, Exeter.

34 At foot of hill, TL into Marshall Road, SP Plym Valley.

35 When road bears right, TL onto cycle track, SP Plym Valley Cycleway (57.5km/35.5 miles). Cross small wooden bridge and pass sewage works on right. Follow SP Plym Valley Cycleway as the track joins short sections of tarmac and passes alongside railway tracks. After 3km (2 miles) cross car park and bear diagonally left. After about 7km (4.5 miles) the track meets a road. TL here and climb very steeply for 200m where TR again, SP (after junction) Goodameavy. Swoop down this road and rejoin cycleway. Continue, through Shaugh Tunnel, to end of cycleway where:

36 TR at TJ, no SP (68.5km/42.5 miles) – TL here to arrive at Skylark Inn. Descend hill and cross weak bridge. Follow SP Cadover Bridge.

37 SO at XR, SP Cadover Bridge (views to left). Follow road round to right, SP Cadover Bridge, and continue along this road across moorland. Cross Cadover Bridge.

38 TL at TJ, SP Wotter/Lee Moor/ Cornwood/Plympton (75km/46.5 miles). Cycle through Wotter and along flat lane into Cornwood. Continue through Cornwood on

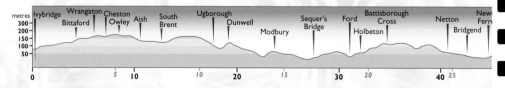

Saltram House

Bond Street, SP Lee Mill/Ivybridge. Cross bridge and pass under railway.

39 TL (effectively SO) along narrow, hedged lane, no SP.

40 TL at roundabout, no SP but other direction SP Ivybridge/Lee Mill (86km/ 53.5 miles). Descend through housing estate.

41 TL at large roundabout, SP Ivybridge/ Bittaford/Ugborough/Tourist Information. TR at roundabout opposite church, into Margerie Kelly Way, SP Bittaford/Station. If you started at the railway station, SO at roundabout, SP Bittaford/Ugborough. Cross zebra crossing and TR at roundabout (opposite Bridge Inn) onto B3213, SP Bittaford/ Ugborough. Continue to station. Otherwise, TL at roundabout, SP Parking/Tourist Information and complete the route. ***88.5km (55 miles)***

Food and drink

Plenty of choice in Ivybridge, South Brent and Modbury. There is a pub and village shop in Holberton and Cornwood, and pubs in many of the villages passed through en route. Refreshments are also available at Saltram House.

Post Office, Bittaford
Post office and convenience store.

Anchor Inn, Ugborough
Bar meals served.

Post Office, Cornwood
Tearoom in the local post office.

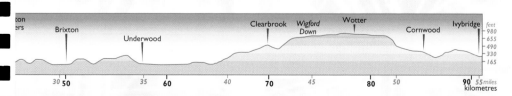

Route information

Distance 93km (58 miles)

Grade Strenuous

Terrain On-road, all the way, with one very short stretch of well-surfaced track. Some steep climbs.

Time to allow 6–10 hours.

Getting there by car Exeter can be accessed from junction 31 of the M5, off the A30 and A377.

Getting there by train Exeter St David's Station is on the main line into the West Country. Telephone (0345) 484950 for information.

Starting at St David's Station in Exeter, the route passes through the centre of Exeter before heading east through Pinhoe. On through a series of pretty villages to Honiton. From here, the route takes you over the scenically splendid Black Down Hills to Dunkeswell. A further collection of villages lead to the Exe Valley and back to Exeter.

Places of interest along the route

A Exeter

The city of Exeter was founded by the Romans almost 2000 years ago and visitors today can still see the huge city walls, constructed around 200AD. There is much to see and do in the city. Exeter once contained over 30 churches and monasteries. **St Peter's Cathedral** was originally constructed by the Normans during the 11th and 12th centuries and largely rebuilt in the 13th century. Among many notable architectural features, the cathedral contains a 15th-century astronomical clock which shows the phases of the moon. **St Nicholas Priory**, the Mint, off Fore Street, was the guest wing of a former Benedictine Priory founded in 1087. It later became an Elizabethan merchant's home. Visitors can see the Norman kitchen, Tudor room and the grand guest hall. Open Easter to October, Monday, Wednesday and Saturday, 1500–1630. Charge. Telephone (01392) 265858. The **Royal Albert Memorial Museum and Art Gallery,** Queen Street, contains displays on local history and archaeology, geology, exotic animals, birds and butterflies, glassware and West Country Silver. Gift shop and tearoom. Open all year, Monday–Saturday 1000–1700. Charge. Telephone (01392) 265858. Exeter contains the country's only Medieval subterranean aqueducts open to the public. The **Underground Passages** are located on Romangate Pass, off the High Street, where visitors can see an exhibition and follow a guided tour. Open October to June, Tuesday–Friday 1400–1645, Saturday 1000–1645; July, August and September, Monday–Saturday 1000–1645. Charge. Telephone (01392) 265887. For further information on Exeter, contact the Tourist Information Centre on (01392) 265700.

B Allhallows Museum, Honiton

Situated in part of the former Allhallows Chapel, dating from the 13th century, and a former

18th-century school dining hall, the museum consists of three galleries. The Norman Gallery exhibits Honiton's most famous product, Honiton Lace, which has been made in the town since 1560, and the Nichol Gallery explains the industry itself with lace-making tools and occasional demonstrations of lace-making. The Murch Gallery illustrates Honiton in prehistoric times and has displays on local industry, schools and costume. Souvenir shop. Open Easter to October, Monday–Saturday 1000–1700 (closed 1600 in October). Charge. Telephone (01404) 44966.

Food and drink

Lots of choice in Exeter and Honiton, and pubs and convenience stores in the villages passed en route.

Otter Inn, near Weston
Pub beside the river. Tea and biscuits served.

The Bomber Café, Dunkeswell
Café on the edge of the airport.

St Peter's Cathedral, Exeter

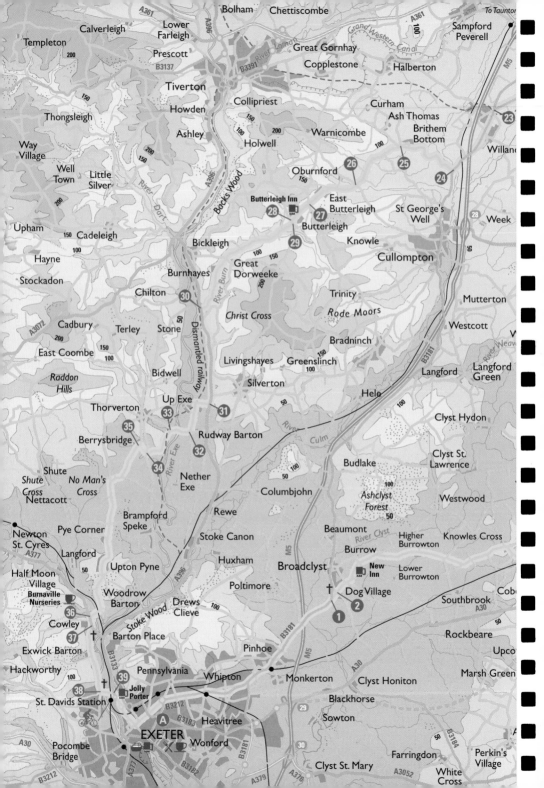

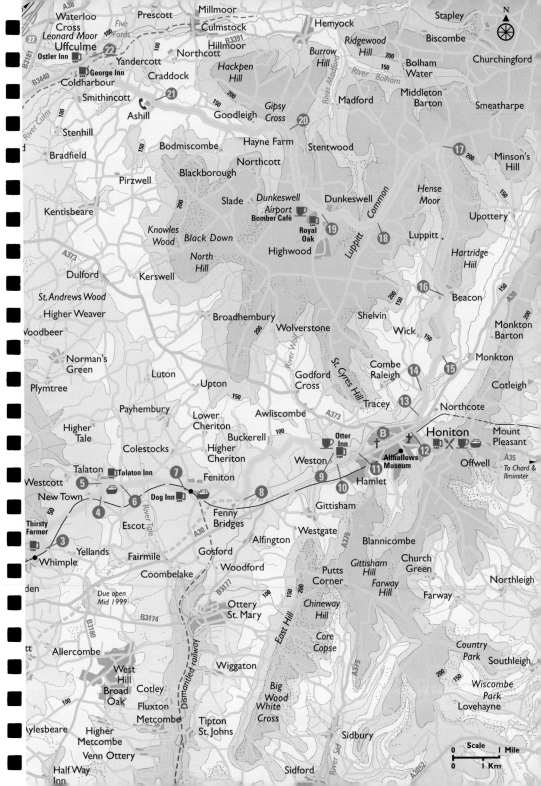

Route description

Leave the station and SO at roundabout (opposite Jolly Porter pub), SP City Centre. Climb St David's Hill. Bear right (effectively SO) at mini round-about, passing Radio Devon on right. Cross a high bridge. SO at XR (traffic lights), SP City Centre, along North Street. At top of the short climb, TL at XR, SP Royal Clarence Hotel Only. Keep SO, following this road as it passes through centre of Exeter, passing Guildhall on left on car-free street (restrictions for cyclists at certain times). SO at traffic lights and ignore road bearing right. Pass Methodist Church on left and cinema on left. SO at large roundabout, SP Pinhoe. Continue through Pinhoe (6.5km/4 miles), following SP for Broadclyst. Cycle towards Broadclyst.

1 TR, SP Whimple/Dog Village.
9.5km (6 miles)

2 TL (effectively SO), SP Whimple. Follow SP Whimple and enter village.

3 TL, SP Talaton and continue into Talaton.

4 TL at TJ, SP Clyst Hydon.
20.5km (12.5 miles)

5 TR, SP Talewater/Feniton.

6 SO at XR (Bittery Cross), SP Talewater/Feniton and continue into Feniton.

7 TL at TJ, no SP. Cross railway. TR, SP Feniton Village and follow tree lined-lane, passing post office on right.

8 TL at Buckerell Cross, SP Buckerell (25.5km/16 miles). Continue through Buckerell and Weston.

9 TR at TJ (Weston Cross), SP Honiton.
30km (18.5 miles)

10 Just before joining A30, TL onto service road and follow this to TL into Honiton.

11 TL at TJ, SP Exeter (avoiding low bridge). Follow SP Town Centre. Allhallows Museum is in the town centre, next to St Paul's Church. Continue through centre of Honiton.

12 TL (effectively SO), SP Chard/Taunton/Ilminster.

13 TL, SP Combe Raleigh/Luppitt/Dunkeswell.

14 TR, no SP. Pass Shaugh Barton and continue.
35.5km (22 miles)

15 LHF. Climb grass-centred, narrow lane.

16 TR at TJ, then TL, SP Upottery. Climb, admiring lovely views on left. At Mathayes Cross follow SP for Hemyock.

17 TL at TJ, SP Dunkeswell/Hemyock/Honiton.
43.5km (27 miles)

18 TR, SP Dunkeswell (light vehicles only).

19 TR at TJ, SP Dunkeswell/Hemyock.
49.5km (31 miles)

20 TL, SP Hayne Farm. Descend a wooded lane and cycle through a ford.
54km (33.5 miles)

21 TR, SP Ashill, (telephone on left). Follow SP Uffculme.

22 TL at TJ (at cemetery corner), SP Uffculme (61km/38 miles). Cycle through Uffculme.

23 TL at TJ, no SP. Continue, following SP Cullompton.
65km (40.5 miles)

24 TR, SP Brithem Bottom/Ash Thomas. Cycle along flat lane into Brithem Bottom.

25 TL, SP Butterleigh.

26 SO at XR (Waymill Cross), SP Butterleigh.
69km (43 miles)

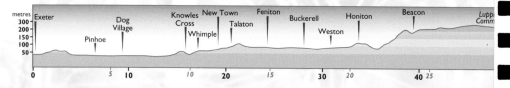

Bickleigh, on the River Exe

27 SO at XR, SP Butterleigh. Enter Butterleigh.

28 TL at TJ, SP Silverton.

29 TR at Force Cross, SP Bickleigh/Bun, along winding lane.

30 TL onto A396, SP Exeter.
76.5km (47.5 miles)

31 TR, SP Up Exe. Follow road through village and bear left. **80km (49.5 miles)**

32 TR at XR (Latchmoor Cross), SP Thorverton. Cross River Exe.

33 TL at Station Cross, no SP. Pass SP Height Restriction and under old railway bridge. Continue along dark wooded lane.

34 TR at TJ, no SP. Immediately TL onto short track.

35 TL at TJ, no SP but adjacent to SP Sharp Bend (83.5km/52 miles). Pass Bembridge House (thatched) on right. Follow SP for Upton Pyne and cycle through village. Cross railway.

36 TL at TJ onto A377, SP Exeter.

37 TR opposite post box, no SP (90km/ 56 miles). Pass SP Width Restriction and then church on left.

38 TL by Parish Church of St Andrew, no SP. Cross River Exe and then the railway.

39 TR at TJ to return to station and complete the route. **93km (58 miles)**

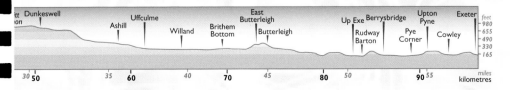

COAST TO COAST – A GRANDE RANDONNÉE

Route information

 Distance 127km (79 miles)

Grade Strenuous

Terrain A wide mixture of road types. Two off-road sections: the first the well-surfaced Camel Trail; the second an indistinct bridleway across Bodmin Moor.

Time to allow 7–12 hours.

Getting there by car Looe is on the south coast of Cornwall, on the A387. There is long term car parking in the town.

Getting there by train There is a railway station at Looe. Telephone (0345) 484950 for information.

This route starts in Looe, a popular touring centre for south east Cornwall and famous for its shark fishing. There is an optional visit to the popular seaside resort at Polperro (adding 6km/4 miles to the distance), before the route heads north through Lostwithiel and into Bodmin. From here you ollow the traffic-free Camel Trail, through Camelford to the attractive coastal town of Boscastle. Then the route runs along the western edge of Bodmin Moor. A final off-road section leads to Jamaica Inn and the return to Looe.

Places of interest along the route

A Lostwithiel

Lostwithiel stands at the head of the River Fowey. **Restormel Castle** was constructed mainly in the 13th century and the remains are administered by English Heritage. There are stunning views from the castle. Open April to October, daily 1000–1800 (dusk if earlier). Charge. Telephone 0171-973 3434 for information. During the Middle Ages Lostwithiel was an important port, processing large quantities of locally produced tin. **Lostwithiel Museum** is housed in the Guildhall, originally the town lock up, and illustrates local history. Large collection of photographs and pictures. For details, telephone Lostwithiel Tourist Information Centre on (01208) 872207.

B Bodmin

Bodmin, once the county town of Cornwall, is at the start of the Camel Trail. **Bodmin Jail Museum**, the former county prison, contains the original dungeons and cells. Also large tearoom and bar. Open all year, daily 1000–1800. Charge. Telephone (01208) 76292. The **Bodmin and Wenford Railway** is located at the restored Bodmin General Station, from where a steam train service is run to Boscarne Junction, to the east of the town. Station buffet. Trains run April to October. Telephone (01208) 73666 for further information.

C Camelford

The town was an important river crossing on the old trade route between Exeter and Launceston, to Wadebridge and Falmouth, and it is said that perhaps Camelford was in fact

King Arthur's Camelot. The award-winning **North Cornwall Museum** illustrates Cornish life over the last century. Exhibits include farming, cider making and a reconstructed moorland cottage. Open April to September, Monday–Saturday 1000–1700. Charge. For further information, telephone Camelford Tourist Information Centre on (01840) 212954.

Ⓓ British Cycling Museum, Camelford

Located in the Old Station at Camelford, the museum illustrates the history of cycling from 1818 to modern times. Huge collection of cycling memorabilia. Open all year, Sunday–Thursday 1000–1700. Charge. Telephone (01840) 212811.

Ⓔ Jamaica Inn, Bolventor

Made famous by Daphne du Maurier's novel, the Jamaica Inn offers a couple of attractions. A tableaux of light and sound illustrates the story and there is also a collection of smug-

Food and drink

There is lots of choice in Looe, Lostwithiel, Bodmin and Camelford, and pubs, cafés and stores in the towns and villages en route. Refreshments are also available at Bodmin Jail Museum, Bodmin and Wenford Railway and the Jamaica Inn.

glers' relics. A memorial room to du Maurier includes her writing desk and other memorabilia. Mr Potter's Museum contains over 10,000 unique exhibits, originally created by Walter Potter, a famous taxidermist. The inn, of course, also welcomes visitors and serves bar and restaurant meals. Exhibitions open February to December, daily 1000–1700. Charge. Telephone (01566) 86025.

Bodmin Moor

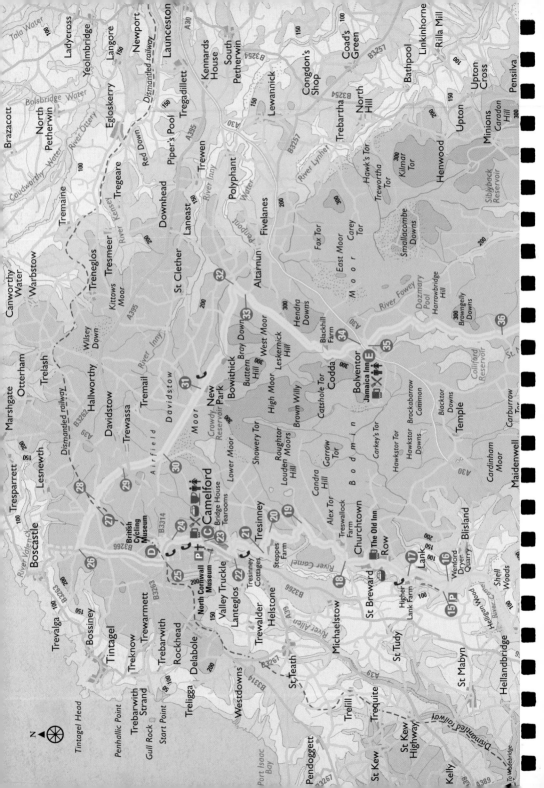

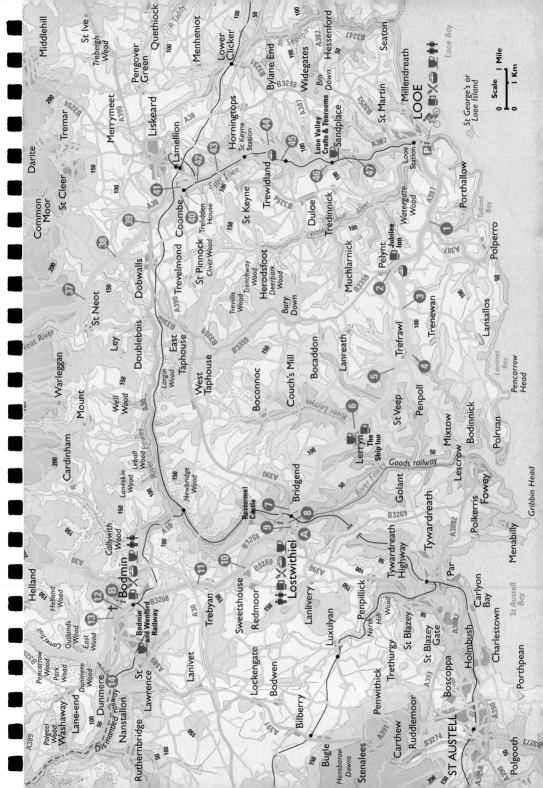

Route description

From the Tourist Information Centre in Looe, go to the bridge to TL onto A387 at TJ. Cross the bridge, following SP Polperro.

1 To visit Polperro, continue on A387 all the way into the village. Otherwise, to continue route, TR, SP Liskeard, Lostwithiel (4km/2.5 miles). Continue to Pelynt.

2 TL, SP Lansallos/Polruan.

3 SO at XR, SP Trefawl/Bodinnick.

4 TR at TJ, SP Lanreath/Liskeard.

11km (7 miles)

5 TL at TJ, SP Bodinnick/Polruan. Immediately TR, SP Lerryn/Highgate. Continue into Lerryn.

6 TR at TJ, SP Lostwithiel/Liskeard (14.5km/9 miles). Cross bridge, leave village and climb. Continue on this undulating road, following SP Lostwithiel.

7 TL at XR into North Street, no SP, and cross railway line and bridge.

8 TL at TJ, SP St Austell.

20.5km (12.5 miles)

9 TR onto B3268 (Tanhouse Road), no SP. Climb through woods and follow SP for Bodmin.

10 TR at TJ, SP Bodmin.

11 SO at roundabout, SP Bodmin (25.5km/16 miles). Cycle into Bodmin, SO at mini roundabout, under railway. Pass Bodmin and Wenford Railway on left. Continue through town.

12 TL at roundabout opposite church, SP Wadebridge.

13 TR along Berrycombe Road for 1km (0.6 mile) and TL onto Camel Trail.

14 TR at TJ, SP Poley's Bridge (30.5km/19 miles). Follow trail all way to end where pass through large car park and leave under height restriction barrier.

15 TR at TJ, no SP (42km/26 miles). Pass Wenford Dryer Quarry on right.

16 TL, SP Lank/St Breward/Camelford. Climb into Penpont. Bear right , SP Lank.

17 TR at TJ opposite Higher Lank Farm, no SP (45km/28 miles). Immediately enter St Breward and continue through village, passing the Old Inn on right.

18 TR on sharp left corner, no SP. Cross cattle grid. Pass Treswallock Farm on right.

19 TL then TL again at TJ, no SP (51.5km/32 miles). Descend then climb steeply.

20 TL at TJ, no SP. Pass Steppes Farm on left and descend.

21 TR at TJ, no SP. Pass Tressinny Cottages on left. Descend and cross bridge.

22 TR at TJ, SP Camelford (56km/35 miles). Descend into town. To visit North Cornwall Museum, TL at Clease Road, then TR following SP Museum. Otherwise, continue through town.

23 Just past car park and church, TL into Trefrew Road.

24 TL at TJ, no SP, and cross Slaughter Bridge. Pass the British Cycle Museum on right.

61km (38 miles)

25 TR at XR, SP Boscastle.

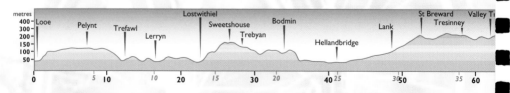

26 To visit Boscastle, follow SP Boscastle down hill. Otherwise, TR at XR, SP Davidstow.

71km (44 miles)

27 TL at TJ, SP Launceston/Davidstow.

28 TR, SP Camelford.

29 SO at XR, across A39 (75.5km/47 miles). Then SO at XR, SP Altarnun. Cross airfield.

30 TL at TJ, SP Altarnun. Continue steady descent, parallel to runways.

31 TR, SP Bowithick (80.5km/50 miles). Cross two fords.

32 Just before bridge, TR, SP Recommended Route for South Carne (85km/53 miles). Pass SP Weight Limit on left.

33 As road bears left, TR onto track, through gate and climb rough track. The bridleway is not well defined, but the following should get you across. Follow track until wall runs out on left (around this point the track bears right, following wall to right). The bridleway you need to follow heads over the small hill in front – in other words, head for smaller hill to right of hill with wall running over summit. Cross gully and cross hill. Wall from hill on left comes down hillside to wooded area at foot – head for this corner. Once there, pass through metal gate in wall and follow another wall on left for 100m. Take RHF uphill, passing post with blue arrow. Follow the now obvious track through gate and over bridge, crossing ford. Tarmac begins at Blackhill Farm.

34 TL at TJ, SP Bodmin (92km/57 miles). Pass under dual carriageway.

35 TL, SP Dozmary Pool/St Neot.

36 TL, SP St Neot/Liskeard. *99km (61.5 miles)*

37 TL at XR (by broken cross), SP Liskeard. Follow road to right, SP Liskeard, and descend into woodland. Cross bridge and climb.

38 SO at XR, no SP but post box on right (105.5km/65.5 miles). Continue along narrow, hedged lane.

39 Where lane comes very close to A38, dismount and go through gap in wall to SO (across A38) at XR, no SP. Pass SP Unsuitable for Long Vehicles. Climb, passing under railway, following SP North Boduel. Descend along narrow lane, close to railway on left.

40 TR at TJ, no SP. Pass Trelidden (house name) on right. TL at TJ opposite Newhouse Farm, no SP. Cross bridge and climb steeply.

41 TR next to Sunnybank (house name), no SP (110km/68.5 miles). Descend to follow a wooded valley parallel to railway.

42 TR at TJ onto two-laned B road, no SP.

43 TL, SP St Keyne Station/Trewidland. Follow the valley, past Trewidland School on right. Climb into Trewidland.

44 TR at TJ, SP Looe. Leave village and descend into valley. Cross bridge.

45 TL at TJ, SP Looe/Sandplace (115km/71.5 miles). Follow the valley and enter Sandplace.

46 TL at TJ (effectively SO), SP Looe/Polperro.

47 TR at TJ, SP Looe/Polperro. Enter Looe, continue past station to Tourist Information Centre and the end of the route.

127km (79 miles)

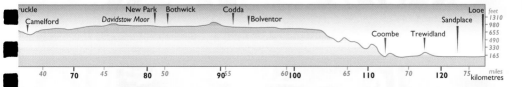

THE CTC

working for cycling

The CTC is Britain's largest national cycling organisation. Founded in 1878, the CTC has over 65,000 members and affiliates throughout the UK, and around 230 local groups. The CTC provides essential services for all leisure cyclists, whether riding on- or off-road, and works to promote cycling and protect cyclists' interests.

Free technical and touring advice

CTC membership makes day-to-day cycling easier. A resident expert cycling engineer answers technical queries about cycle buying, maintenance and equipment. And if you get ambitious about your cycling, the CTC's Touring Department has reams of information about cycling anywhere from Avon to Zimbabwe. Then, when it comes to getting kitted out, the CTC's mail order shop sells a wide variety of clothing and accessories in addition to books, maps and guidebooks, including other titles from HarperCollins.

CTC Helpdesk – telephone (01483) 417217

CTC members also receive *Cycle Touring and Campaigning* magazine free six times a year. *CT&C* takes pride in its journalistic independence. With reports on cycle trips all over the globe, forensic tests on bikes and equipment, and the most vigorous and effective pro-bike campaigning stance anywhere, *CT&C* is required reading for any cyclist.

CTC membership costs from £15 p.a.

It is not just members who benefit. The CTC works on behalf of all Britain's 22 million cycle owners. Its effective campaigning at national level helped to create the Government's National Cycling Strategy. It is lobbying for lower speed limits on country lanes; campaigning so that you can carry bikes on trains; working with Local Authorities to make towns more cycle-friendly, to ensure that roads are designed to meet cyclists' needs and kept well maintained; making sure that bridleways are kept open; and negotiating cyclists' access to canal towpaths.

Whatever kind of cyclist you are – mountain biker, Sunday potterer, bicycle commuter, or out for the day with your family – cycling is easier and safer with the CTC's knowledge and services in your saddlebag. The CTC is the essential accessory for every cyclist!

For further information contact:
CTC
69 Meadrow
Godalming
Surrey
GU7 3HS

Telephone (01483) 417217
Fax (01483) 426994
e-mail: cycling@ctc.org.uk
Website: http://www.ctc.org.uk